JULIUS CAESAR

Edited by
Maurice Charney
Rutgers University

THE PERFECTION FORM COMPANY
LOGAN, IOWA

A NOTE FROM THE PUBLISHER

The purpose of the Parallel Text Series of Shakespeare's plays is to assist the reader in understanding and appreciating the work of the foremost poet and dramatist of the English language. That there are considerable difficulties in reading and understanding this language is apparent from a casual glance through the many modern editions of the plays, which are accompanied by copious notes on each page of the text. Even these heavily annotated editions often fail to go far enough in illuminating the richly poetic and elliptical language that in large part demonstrates Shakespeare's genius and primacy, and constitutes our frequent perplexity.

In providing a line-by-line, contemporary prose paraphrase of the play on facing pages we have, in a sense, merely carried the convention of using explanatory notes to its logical conclusion. No attempt has been made to translate Shakespeare into modern poetry — a presumptuous and virtually impossible task. Instead, we have tried to render the often unfamiliar and remote Elizabethan language into a neutral and comprehensible modern equivalent. By its very nature, this task sometimes neglects the richness and complexity of the text, which is, in part, created by Shakespeare's magnificent and original use of language. Thus, the paraphrase is offered as an aid to understanding, not as a substitute for reading the original. The reader will find that referring to the paraphrase will often clarify the surface of the text, but the rewards to be found in reading Shakespeare yield themselves only to the careful and dedicated student of the original.

The Past is Prologue

Shakespeare lives! So writes his most eminent biographer, S. Schoenbaum, in the prologue to *Shakespeare: The Globe and the World* (New York: Oxford University Press, 1979). And the evidence is all around us.

We find it in the language we use. When we lament that "the course of true love never did run smooth," whether we are conscious of it or not, we are quoting from *A Midsummer Night's Dream*. When we observe that a well-intended law or regulation is "more honor'd in the breach than the observance," we are applying — or perhaps misapplying — a phrase from *Hamlet*. When we inscribe "What's past is prologue" on the National Archives building in our nation's capital, we are dignifying a minor line from *The Tempest*. Often without realizing it, we find ourselves speaking, if only momentarily, in the accents of a Portia or a Polonius, a Macbeth or a Mercutio. And when we *do* realize it — when we are conscious of the Shakespearean idiom embedded in so much of our daily speech — we take pleasure in those subtle turns of phrase that continue to enrich our discourse. A veteran gardener recently observed, for example, that anyone who calls a rose by any other name has probably been pruning.

Alongside the Greek classics and the King James version of the Bible, Shakespeare's words and works offer a cultural treasure chest from which English-speaking peoples have been drawing, in one way or another, for more than three and a half centuries. Folks have been

following the advice given in *Kiss Me Kate* —
brushing up on their Shakespeare — for quite
some time.

But Shakespeare's presence is also reflected in
a number of other ways. Consider, for example,
the more than 800 operatic and symphonic com-
positions deriving from such plays as *The Merry
Wives of Windsor*, *The Taming of the Shrew*, and
Othello. Or Broadway musicals, such as *The Boys
from Syracuse* (a take-off on *The Comedy of
Errors*) and *West Side Story* (Leonard Bernstein's
New York gang-war updating of *Romeo and
Juliet*). Or literary works such as William
Faulkner's *The Sound and the Fury*, a sustained
allusion to Macbeth's "tomorrow and tomorrow
and tomorrow" speech. Here in the United
States, Shakespeare has been part of our lives
since the earliest days of the republic — even on
the frontier, where spinoffs and parodies of
Shakespeare helped while away many an hour in
the nineteenth century. We've all delighted in the
fractured Shakespeare offered up by the Duke
and the King in Mark Twain's *Huckleberry Finn*.
Ah yes, numerous — but not always sweet — are
the uses of Shakespeare.

Nor is there any reason to think that
Shakespeare's influence will be any less vital in
the future than in the past. In most of the countries of the world, Shakespeare continues to maintain his position as the most frequently
performed playwright. Every summer in the
United States, for example, Shakespeare festivals
highlight the vacation map from Maine to Texas,
from Alabama to Oregon.

Ben Jonson was right, then, when he prefaced
the first collected edition of Shakespeare's plays
with the words "he was not of an age, but for all
time!"

The Stratford Years

But if Shakespeare was a man for all time, he
was also very much a man of his own age.
Christened at Holy Trinity Church in Stratford-
upon-Avon in April, 1564, he grew up, the son of
illiterate parents, in a small Warwickshire town
more noted for its wool and leather goods than
for its literary cultivation. His mother, Mary
Arden, was the daughter of a well-to-do farmer.
His father, John Shakespeare, was a successful
glovemaker who held several important borough
offices in Stratford before he suffered financial
reverses during William's teen years. The birth-
place house still stands.

It seems all but certain that young Shakespeare
spent most of his weekdays at the nearby
Stratford grammar school, where, having learned
his ABCs and the Lord's Prayer from a horn-
book, he would have gone on to study Latin

Holy Trinity Church, Stratford-on-Avon

Shakespeare's House, Stratford-on-Avon

under the supervision of a stern schoolmaster.
Sundays he would have attended religious
services, studying the catechism of the newly
re-established Church of England and worshiping
in accordance with *The Book of Common Prayer*.

It was a rigorous upbringing, and it equipped
Shakespeare with enough background to become
one of the most widely educated men who ever
lived — despite the fact that he never attended a
day at a college or university.

Judging from his plays and poems, we may
infer that Shakespeare was interested in virtually
every aspect of human life — in professions such
as law, medicine, religion, and teaching; in everyday occupations such as farming, sheepherding,
tailoring, and shopkeeping; in skills such as
fishing, gardening, and cooking. Much of what
Shakespeare knew about these and countless
other subjects he would have acquired from
books. He must have been a voracious reader.

But he would have learned a great deal, also, from simply being alert to all that went on around him. He would have observed the plant and animal life of the nearby woods that he would later immortalize, in *As You Like It*, as the Forest of Arden. While there, he may have hunted from time to time; one legend has it that he left Stratford because he had been caught poaching deer from the estate of a powerful squire four miles upstream. He probably learned to swim as a youth, skinny-dipping in the river Avon. He may have participated in the kinds of athletic competition that were popular in the Elizabethan equivalent of the Olympics, the Cotswold Games. Chances are, too, that he would have been familiar with indoor recreations such as hazard (a popular dice game), or chess, or any of a number of card games. His works make it clear that he was fully at home with a broad spectrum of pastimes characteristic of the daily life of Elizabethan England.

Once his schooldays ended, Shakespeare married, at the age of eighteen, a woman who was eight years his senior. Anne Hathaway was pregnant when the wedding vows were solemnized. That it was a forced marriage is unlikely. But we shall never know how close the couple were. What we do know is that a daughter, Susanna, was baptized in Holy Trinity in May of 1583, followed less than two years later by the christening of twins, Hamnet and Judith. Sometime thereafter, certainly by the late 1580s, the father was in London.

The London Years

London was approximately a hundred miles distant. Shakespeare may have traveled there by way of the spires of Oxford, as do most visitors returning from Stratford to London today. But why he went, or when, history does not tell us. It has been plausibly suggested that he joined an acting troupe that was one player short when it toured Stratford in 1587. All we know for certain is that by 1592 Shakespeare had established himself as an actor and had written at least three plays. One of these — the third part of *Henry VI* — was alluded to in that year in a testament by a dying poet and playwright. Robert Greene warned his fellow playwrights to beware of the "upstart crow" who, not content with being a mere player, was aspiring to a share of the livelihood that had previously been the exclusive province of professional writers such as "the University Wits."

If we look at what Shakespeare had written by the early 1590s, we see that he had already become thoroughly familiar with the daily round of what was rapidly developing into one of the great capitals of Europe. Shakespeare knew St. Paul's Cathedral, famous not only as a house of worship but also as the marketplace where books were bought and sold. He knew the Inns of Court, where aspiring young lawyers studied for the bar. He knew the river Thames,

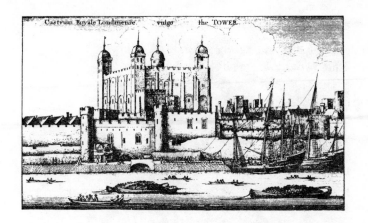

Castrum Royale Londinense   vulgo   the TOWER.

spanned by the ever-busy, ever-fascinating
London Bridge. He knew the Tower, where so
many of the characters he would depict in his
history plays had met their deaths, and where in
his own lifetime, such prominent noblemen as the
Earl of Essex and Sir Walter Raleigh would be
imprisoned prior to their executions. He knew
Westminster, where Parliament met when sum-
moned by the Queen, and where the Queen
herself kept her court at Whitehall Palace. He
knew the harbor, where English ships, having
won control of the seas by defeating the "invincible" Spanish Armada in 1588, had begun in
earnest to explore the New World.

In Shakespeare's day, London was a vigorous
city of approximately 160,000. If in its more
majestic aspects it was dominated by the court of
Queen Elizabeth — the sovereign most historians
regard as the greatest monarch in English
history — in its everyday affairs it was accented
by the hustle-bustle of getting and spending. Its
Royal Exchange was one of the forerunners of
today's stock exchanges. Its many marketplaces
offered a variety of goods for a variety of tastes.

Its crowded streets presented a colorful pageant of Elizabethan modes of transport and dress, ranging from countrywomen in homespun to elegant ladies in apparel as decorative as their husbands' wealth — and the Queen's edicts on clothing — would allow. Its inns and taverns afforded a robust diversity of vivid personalities—eating, drinking, talking, and enjoying games of all kinds.

London was, in short, a stimulating social and cultural environment for the poet whose works would later be praised as the very "mirror of life." And the young playwright took full advantage of the opportunity to observe humanity in all its facets. Without the broadening that London provided, it is doubtful that Shakespeare could ever have created such breathtakingly real characters as Falstaff, Prince Hal, and "all the good lads in Eastcheap."

Not that all was always well. Like any major city, London also had its unpleasant aspects. For one thing, it was riddled with conflict. Preachers were constantly denouncing the excessive use of cosmetics by women of the period. Even Hamlet speaks out against "your paintings," telling Ophelia "God has given you one face, and you make yourselves another."

In a similar vein, the city's Puritan authorities, regarding the theatres as dens of iniquity, closed them down on any available pretext, particularly during periods when the plague was rampant.

But even with the theatres closed, London was not free of vice and crime. In the Bankside district, prostitution abounded, as did gambling and drunkenness. Pickpockets, vagabonds, and other members of the fraternity of urban lowlife lay in wait for "conies" or unsuspecting victims. With so many "notorious villainies" for the "Belman of London" to bring to light, it is not surprising that some of the most interesting pamphlets of the period were muckraking tracts from reformers outraged by the sinfulness of the modern metropolis.

In such a setting did Shakespeare write and perform the greatest dramatic works the world has ever seen. And he did so in an area of the city that was accustomed to entertainments we would regard as the very antithesis of the sweet Swan of Avon's poetic sublimity. For if Bankside was to blossom into the finest theatrical center of that or any other age, it was also, for better or worse, the seedbed for such crude and cruel spectator sports as bear-baiting, bull-baiting, and cock-fighting. This may help account for the blood and violence one often sees on the Elizabethan stage, even in such Shakespearean works as *Titus Andronicus*, *Julius Caesar*, and *King Lear*.

But of course there was more than murder and mayhem in the "wooden O" that served as amphitheatre for Shakespeare's works. On a stage largely devoid of scenery, the playwright and the actor made splendid use of language and gesture to establish locale, atmosphere, and meaning. And because the stage was surrounded on three sides by nearby spectators, the playwright and the actor benefited from a more intimate relationship with the audience than is customary in present-day theatres fitted with a curtain and a proscenium arch. For Shakespeare, this meant that he could allow a character to con-fide in the audience through asides, as does Iago in *Othello*, or to be overheard as he meditates in solitude, as does Hamlet in his celebrated "To be or not to be" soliloquy.

The limitations of the Globe and similar Elizabethan theatres are obvious to us today. For one thing, they were exposed to the sky and thus could not operate comfortably in inclement weather or in darkness. For another, lacking spotlights and other modern paraphernalia, they could not achieve some of the special effects we have come to take for granted in the theatre of our own day. What we sometimes forget, however, is that these limitations could be liberating for the playwright and the actor, making possible a kind of dramatic invention and flexibility difficult to duplicate in the more "advanced" theatre of the twentieth century.

The same was probably true in the Blackfriars and other private indoor theatres of the period, not to mention the halls at Court or the great palaces of the nobility. For it is well to remember that many of Shakespeare's plays were performed in theatrical settings other than the Globe, or its predecessor, the Theatre, or other amphitheatres of the period. Shakespeare's company was known as the Lord Chamberlain's Men from 1594 to 1603, when Queen Elizabeth died; after the accession of King James I, from 1603 on, it was known as the King's Men. Both designations implied a special relationship with the Court, and Shakespeare and his colleagues were invited to perform before the monarch more often than all the other acting troupes in the realm combined.

Shakespeare's real bread and butter, however, came from the immense cross section of the English populace who thronged to Bankside to see his plays performed. Despite the occasional caviling of such rival playwrights as Ben Jonson (whose admiration for Shakespeare was at times "this side idolatry"), we have reason to believe

Interior of Holy Trinity Church

that Shakespeare's dramatic works were immediately recognized for their artistic merits. By 1598, a critic named Francis Meres was comparing Shakespeare's genius to that of the greatest poets of antiquity — Ovid, Plautus, and Seneca — and finding the contemporary playwright superior to his classical predecessors. But unlike many great writers, Shakespeare was also a popular success in his own lifetime. He earned a generous amount of money, invested it wisely in real estate, both in London and in Stratford, and around 1613, eased into a gentleman's retirement — the owner of New Place, the second largest house in his native town.

There, three years later, he died. Fittingly, his death date, like the date tradition has agreed upon for his birth date, was April 23, the day England celebrated its patron saint. In the four centuries since the poet's birth, it seems no exaggeration to say that he has eclipsed even the heroic St. George in glory.

Epilogue

Shakespeare was laid to rest where fifty-two years earlier he had been christened. Shortly thereafter, a monument to his memory was erected above the tomb in Holy Trinity, and that monument is still in place for Shakespeare admirers to see today. But an even greater monument to his memory was produced several years later, when his theatrical colleagues assembled a large volume of his plays. The First Folio of 1623 was a labor of love, compiled as "an office to the dead, to procure his orphans' guardians" and "to keep the memory of so worthy a friend and fellow alive as was our Shakespeare." To that end, it was an unparalleled success, a publication that has aptly been summed up as "incomparably the most important work in the English language."

Among other things, the First Folio preserves what is generally considered the most reliable portrait of Shakespeare, the title-page engraving by Martin Droeshout. In dedicatory verses opposite the portrait, Ben Jonson attests to its authenticity. But quite properly, he then goes on to observe that though the engraver has "hit his face," he has been unable to draw "his wit." For that — for the mastery of language, of character, of poetic drama, of all that reminds us that, after all is said and done, "the play's the thing" — Jonson tells the reader, "look not on his picture but his book."

And so, for more than three and a half centuries, we have. We have read, and studied, and memorized, and performed — and yes, we have worshiped — the man Jonson praised as "Soul of the Age! The applause, delight, the wonder of our stage!"

Bardolatry — the word we use to refer to Shakespeare-worship — has had many manifestations over the intervening centuries. It has animated hundreds of Shakespeare festivals and celebrations, of which undoubtedly the most famous was the great Shakespeare Jubilee of 1769. On that occasion, thousands braved rainy Stratford weather to participate in ceremonies presided over by the principal actor of the eighteenth century, David Garrick. In a somewhat inverted form, Bardolatry has given rise to the notion that someone other than the son of ill-educated, small-town parents wrote the plays we attribute to William Shakespeare. Hence Francis Bacon, the Earl of Oxford, and other members of the nobility have been proposed as the "true" author of the works we still securely hold to be Shakespeare's. And Bardolatry has also occasioned an unceasing cavalcade of Shakespearean curios and knickknacks: everything from ceramic figurines and mulberry-wood chests to Shakespeare-lovers' poker cloths and Superbard T-shirts.

On the more serious side, appreciation of Shakespeare has inspired notable works of art by painters as diverse as Thomas Rowlandson, George Romney, Henry Fuseli, Eugene Delacroix, George Cruikshank, Arthur Rackham, Pablo Picasso, Salvador Dali, and David Hockney. His works have provided the basis of hundreds of musical tributes, by composers ranging from Beethoven to Mendelssohn, Tchaikovsky to Verdi. And of course his plays continue to be performed in theatres, in movie houses, and on television screens.

The Bard is in our bones. Shakespeare lives.

John F. Andrews
Former Editor Shakespeare Quarterly
Folger Shakespeare Library

GOOD FREND FOR IESVS SAKE FORBEARE
TO DIGG THE DVST ENCLOASED HEARE
BLESE BE Y MAN Y SPARES HES STONE
AND CVRST BE HE Y MOVES MY BONES

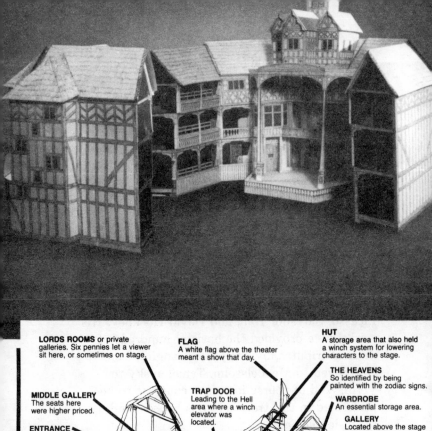

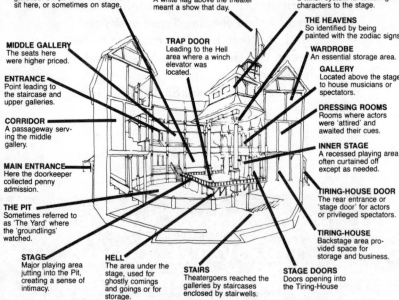

LORDS ROOMS or private galleries. Six pennies let a viewer sit here, or sometimes on stage.

FLAG
A white flag above the theater meant a show that day.

HUT
A storage area that also held a winch system for lowering characters to the stage.

MIDDLE GALLERY
The seats here were higher priced.

TRAP DOOR
Leading to the Hell area where a winch elevator was located.

THE HEAVENS
So identified by being painted with the zodiac signs.

WARDROBE
An essential storage area.

ENTRANCE
Point leading to the staircase and upper galleries.

GALLERY
Located above the stage to house musicians or spectators.

CORRIDOR
A passageway serving the middle gallery.

DRESSING ROOMS
Rooms where actors were 'attired' and awaited their cues.

MAIN ENTRANCE
Here the doorkeeper collected penny admission.

INNER STAGE
A recessed playing area often curtained off except as needed.

THE PIT
Sometimes referred to as 'The Yard' where the 'groundlings' watched.

TIRING-HOUSE DOOR
The rear entrance or 'stage door' for actors or privileged spectators.

TIRING-HOUSE
Backstage area provided space for storage and business.

STAGE
Major playing area jutting into the Pit, creating a sense of intimacy.

HELL
The area under the stage, used for ghostly comings and goings or for storage.

STAIRS
Theatergoers reached the galleries by staircases enclosed by stairwells.

STAGE DOORS
Doors opening into the Tiring-House

JULIUS CAESAR

Marlon Brando as Antony. From the MGM release *Julius Caesar*
© 1953, Loew's Incorporated.

The Tragedy of
Julius Caesar

Act I, Scene i: [*Rome, a street*]. *Enter* FLAVIUS, MURELLUS, *and certain Commoners over the stage.*

FLAVIUS
    Hence! Home, you idle creatures, get you home.
    Is this a holiday? What, know you not,
    Being mechanical, you ought not walk
    Upon a laboring day without the sign
5   Of your profession? Speak, what trade art thou?

CARPENTER
    Why, sir, a carpenter.

MURELLUS
    Where is thy leather apron and thy rule?
    What dost thou with thy best apparel on?
    You, sir, what trade are you?

COBBLER
10   Truly, sir, in respect of a fine workman, I am but, as you would
    say, a cobbler.

MURELLUS
    But what trade art thou? Answer me directly.

COBBLER
    A trade, sir, that I hope I may use with a safe conscience, which
    is indeed, sir, a mender of bad soles.*

MURELLUS
15   What trade, thou knave? Thou naughty knave, what trade?

---

14 *soles*   wordplay on "soles-souls."

The Tragedy of
Julius Caesar

Act I. Scene i: A street in Rome. Enter the Tribunes FLAVIUS *and* MURELLUS *at one side of the stage, and, at the other, a group of ordinary citizens, who walk across the stage toward the Tribunes.*

FLAVIUS

    Go away! Go home, you lazy creatures, get back to your homes!
    Is today a holiday? What, don't you know that,
    being workingmen, you shouldn't walk around
    on a working day without your work clothes

5   and tools? Speak up, what's your trade?

CARPENTER

    Why, sir, a carpenter.

MURELLUS

    Where's your leather apron and your carpenter's ruler?
    What are you doing with your best clothes on?
    You, sir, what's your trade?

SHOEMAKER

    Indeed, sir, in comparison with a fine workman, I am only,

10   as you would
    say, a shoemaker.

MURELLUS

    But what's your trade? Answer me without beating
      around the bush.

SHOEMAKER

    A trade sir, that I hope I may practice with a
      good conscience, which
    is indeed, sir, a mender of bad soles.

MURELLUS (*becoming more and more annoyed at the*
    Shoemaker's wordplay)

15   What trade, you villain? You worthless faker, what trade?

COBBLER

Nay, I beseech you, sir, be not out with me; yet if you be out, sir, I can mend you.

MURELLUS

What mean'st thou by that? Mend me, thou saucy fellow?

COBBLER

Why, sir, cobble you.

FLAVIUS

20   Thou art a cobbler, art thou?

COBBLER

Truly, sir, all that I live by is with the awl. I meddle with no tradesman's matters nor women's matters; but withal* I am indeed, sir, a surgeon to old shoes. When they are in great danger, I recover* them. As proper men as ever trod upon neat's leather
25   have gone upon my handiwork.

FLAVIUS

But wherefore art not in thy shop today?
Why dost thou lead these men about the streets?

COBBLER

Truly, sir, to wear out their shoes, to get myself into more work. But indeed, sir, we make holiday to see Caesar and to rejoice in
30   his triumph.

MURELLUS

Wherefore rejoice? What conquest brings he home?
What tributaries follow him to Rome
To grace in captive bonds his chariot wheels?
You blocks, you stones, you worse than senseless things!
35   O you hard hearts, you cruel men of Rome,
Knew you not Pompey*? Many a time and oft
Have you climbed up to walls and battlements,
To towers and windows, yea, to chimney tops,
Your infants in your arms, and there have sat
40   The livelong day, with patient expectation,
To see great Pompey pass the streets of Rome.

---

22 *withal* wordplay on "with awl," "with all," and "withal" (= "nevertheless").

24 *recover* wordplay on "re-sole" and "make well."

SHOEMAKER

> I beg of you, sir, don't be angry with me. But if you're either
>   out of temper or out at heels,
> I can fix you up.

MURELLUS

> What do you mean by that? "Fix me up," you impudent rascal?

SHOEMAKER

> Why, sir, fix your shoes.

FLAVIUS

20
> You are a shoemaker, aren't you?

SHOEMAKER

> Indeed, sir, all that I make my living by is with my shoemaker's
>   awl. I don't fool around with any
> businessman's matters or with any woman's matters,
>   but still I am indeed,
> sir, a surgeon to old shoes. When they are in great danger
>   for their life,
> I heal them. As handsome men as ever walked on cow's leather
25
> have walked in my hand-made shoes.

FLAVIUS

> But why aren't you in your shop today?
> Why are you leading these men about with you in the streets?

SHOEMAKER

> Truly, sir, to wear out their shoes, in order to make
>   work for myself.
> But indeed, sir, we are taking a holiday to see Caesar
>   and to rejoice in
30
> his victory procession.

MURELLUS

> Why rejoice? What spoils does he bring home with him?
> What rich captives for ransom follow him to Rome
> to do honor, even in their chains, to his chariot wheels?
> You blockheads, you men of stone—worse than creatures
>   deprived of their five senses!
35
> O you hard-hearted people, you cruel men of Rome,
> didn't you know Pompey the Great? You often
> climbed up walls and fortifications,
> to towers and windows, even to chimney tops,
> your infants in your arms, and sat there
40
> all day long, with patient expectation,
> to see great Pompey pass by in the streets of Rome.

---

36 *Pompey* Pompey the Great, who was defeated by Caesar in civil war
in 48 B.C. and later murdered.

And when you saw his chariot but appear,
Have you not made an universal shout,
That Tiber trembled underneath her banks
45   To hear the replication of your sounds
Made in her concave shores?
And do you now put on your best attire?
And do you now cull out a holiday?
And do you now strew flowers in his way
50   That comes in triumph over Pompey's blood?
Be gone!
Run to your houses, fall upon your knees,
Pray to the gods to intermit the plague
That needs must light on this ingratitude.
FLAVIUS
55   Go, go, good countrymen, and for this fault
Assemble all the poor men of your sort;
Draw them to Tiber banks, and weep your tears
Into the channel, till the lowest stream
Do kiss the most exalted shores of all.
Exeunt all the Commoners.
60   See whe'r their basest mettle be not moved;
They vanish tongue-tied in their guiltiness.
Go you down that way towards the Capitol;
This way will I. Disrobe the images,
If you do find them decked with ceremonies.
MURELLUS
65   May we do so?
You know it is the feast of Lupercal.*
FLAVIUS
It is no matter; let no images
Be hung with Caesar's trophies. I'll about
And drive away the vulgar from the streets.
70   So do you too, where you perceive them thick.
These growing feathers plucked from Caesar's wing
Will make him fly an ordinary pitch,
Who else would soar above the view of men
And keep us all in servile fearfulness.
Exeunt.

---

66 *feast of Lupercal* an ancient Roman fertility festival held on February 15 in honor of Lupercus, an Italian equivalent of the god Pan.

And when you saw his chariot appear,
didn't you all cheer so powerfully
that the Tiber River trembled within her banks
45   to hear your mighty sounds
echo within her overhanging shores?
And do you now get all dressed up?
And do you now pick out a holiday for yourselves?
And do you now throw flowers in Caesar's path,
50   who comes fresh from his victory over Pompey's sons?
Get away!
Run to your houses, fall on your knees,
and pray to the gods to prevent the plague
that must surely fall on you to punish your ingratitude.

FLAVIUS
55   Go, go, my fellow countrymen, and to atone for this misdeed,
assemble all the poor workingmen.
Lead them to the banks of the Tiber and weep your tears
into the river until the lowest stream fills up and
kisses the top of its enclosing banks.
     Exit all the common people.
60   See if their worthless character isn't moved by what I've said.
They vanish speechless in their feelings of guilt.
You go down that way towards the Capitol;
I'll go this way. Strip the statues put up for Caesar's celebration
if you find them decked out with festive adornments.

MURELLUS
65   Is it legal?
You know that it is now the feast of Lupercal.

FLAVIUS
It doesn't matter—don't let any statues
be hung with Caesar's triumphal ornaments. Meanwhile,
     I'll go around
and drive the ordinary citizens out of the streets.
70   You do the same where you see them gathered in groups.
If we can pluck these growing feathers out of Caesar's wing,
we can force him to fly lower.
Otherwise, he will soar out of sight
and keep us all in slavish fear.
     They exit.

[*Scene ii: Rome, a public place.*] *Enter* CAESAR, ANTONY (*for the course**), CALPHURNIA, PORTIA, DECIUS, CICERO, BRUTUS, CASSIUS, CASCA, *a Soothsayer,* [*and citizens*]. *After them,* MURELLUS *and* FLAVIUS.

CAESAR
  Calphurnia.

CASCA
                Peace, ho! Caesar speaks.

CAESAR
                                Calphurnia.

CALPHURNIA
  Here, my lord.

CAESAR
  Stand you directly in Antonio's way
  When he doth run his course. Antonio.

ANTONY
5 Caesar, my lord.

CAESAR
  Forget not in your speed, Antonio,
  To touch Calphurnia; for our elders say,
    The barren, touchèd in this holy chase,
  Shake off their sterile curse.

ANTONY
                    I shall remember.
10 When Caesar says, "Do this," it is performed.

CAESAR
  Set on, and leave no ceremony out.

SOOTHSAYER
  Caesar!

CAESAR
  Ha! Who calls?

CASCA
  Bid every noise be still. Peace yet again.

CAESAR
  Who is it in the press that calls on me?
  I hear a tongue shriller than all the music
  Cry "Caesar!" Speak; Caesar is turned to hear.

---

  for the course foot races were part of the celebration of the Lupercalia (see note at 1.1.66). Plutarch tells us that men "run naked through the city,

Scene ii: A public place in Rome. Enter CAESAR, ANTONY *(dressed for running),* CALPHURNIA, PORTIA, DECIUS, CICERO, BRUTUS, CASSIUS, CASCA, *a Fortune-Teller, and Roman citizens. Following them,* MURELLUS *and* FLAVIUS.

CAESAR
Calphurnia.

CASCA
Quiet there! Caesar speaks.

CAESAR
Calphurnia.

CALPHURNIA
Here, my lord.

CAESAR
Stand alongside the path Antonio will take
when he is running. Antonio.

ANTONY
5   Caesar, my lord.

CAESAR
When you're speeding by, Antonio, don't forget
to touch Calphurnia, because our wise men say that
barren women, when touched in this holy race,
are able to shake off the curse of sterility.

ANTONY
I shall remember.
10   When Caesar says, "Do this," it is done.

CAESAR
Proceed, and don't leave out any part of the ceremony.

FORTUNE-TELLER
Caesar!

CAESAR
What! Who calls?

CASCA
Let every sound be still. Silence once again.

CAESAR
15   Who in the crowd calls me?
I hear a tongue more piercing than all the music
cry "Caesar!" Speak; Caesar has turned to hear you.

---

striking in sport them they meet in their way with leather thongs, hair and all on, to make them give place."

SOOTHSAYER
Beware the ides of March.*
CAESAR
                              What man is that?
BRUTUS
A soothsayer bids you beware the ides of March.
CAESAR
Set him before me; let me see his face.
CASSIUS
Fellow, come from the throng; look upon Caesar.
CAESAR
What say'st thou to me now? Speak once again.
SOOTHSAYER
Beware the ides of March.
CAESAR
He is a dreamer; let us leave him. Pass.
          Sennet. Exeunt. BRUTUS *and* CASSIUS *remain.*
CASSIUS
25   Will you go see the order of the course?
BRUTUS
Not I.
CASSIUS
I pray you do.
BRUTUS
I am not gamesome; I do lack some part
Of that quick spirit that is in Antony.
30   Let me not hinder, Cassius, your desires.
I'll leave you.
CASSIUS
Brutus, I do observe you now of late.
I have not from your eyes that gentleness
And show of love as I was wont to have.
35   You bear too stubborn and too strange a hand
Over your friend that loves you.
BRUTUS
                              Cassius,
Be not deceived. If I have veiled my look,
I turn the trouble of my countenance
Merely upon myself. Vexèd I am

---

18 *ides of March*   March 15. According to the Roman calendar, the ides
were the mid-point of the month: the fifteenth day in March, May, July, and
October, and the thirteenth day in all other months.

FORTUNE-TELLER

Beware the ides of March.

CAESAR

Who is that?

BRUTUS

A fortune-teller who warns you to beware the ides of March.

CAESAR

20 Bring him before me; let me see his face.

CASSIUS

Fellow, come here from out of the crowd; look at Caesar.

CAESAR

What do you say to me now? Speak again.

FORTUNE-TELLER

Beware the ides of March.

CAESAR

He is a dreamer; let us leave him. Go on.

A flourish of trumpets. All exit except BRUTUS *and*
CASSIUS.

CASSIUS

25 Are you going to watch the races?

BRUTUS

Not I.

CASSIUS

I beg you to go.

BRUTUS

I am not fond of sports. I lack some
of that lively spirit that Antony has.
30 Don't let me stop you, Cassius, from doing what you want to.
I'll leave you.

CASSIUS

Brutus, I've been observing you lately.
I don't see that gentleness
and show of affection in your eyes that I used to receive from you.
35 You have too harsh and too distant a manner
with your friend who loves you.

BRUTUS

Cassius,
don't be deceived by appearances. If my looks seem to you
unfriendly,
it is because my troubled face is turned
only to my own problems. I have been upset

40   Of late with passions of some difference,
      Conceptions only proper to myself,
      Which give some soil, perhaps, to my behaviors.
      But let not therefore my good friends be grieved
      (Among which number, Cassius, be you one),
45   Nor construe any further my neglect
      Than that poor Brutus, with himself at war,
      Forgets the shows of love to other men.

CASSIUS
      Then, Brutus, I have much mistook your passion,
      By means whereof this breast of mine hath buried
50   Thoughts of great value, worthy cogitations.
      Tell me, good Brutus, can you see your face?

BRUTUS
      No, Cassius;
      For the eye sees not itself but by reflection,
      By some other things.

CASSIUS
                        'Tis just.
      And it is very much lamented, Brutus,
      That you have no such mirrors as will turn
      Your hidden worthiness into your eye,
      That you might see your shadow. I have heard
      Where many of the best respect in Rome—
      Except immortal Caesar—speaking of Brutus,
      And groaning underneath this age's yoke,
      Have wished that noble Brutus had his eyes.

BRUTUS
      Into what dangers would you lead me, Cassius,
      That you would have me seek into myself
65   For that which is not in me?

CASSIUS
      Therefore, good Brutus, be prepared to hear.
      And since you know you cannot see yourself
      So well as by reflection, I, your glass,
      Will modestly discover to yourself
70   That of yourself which you yet know not of.
      And be not jealous on me, gentle Brutus.

40   recently with conflicting emotions,
thoughts that I must keep to myself,
which perhaps have a harmful effect on my behavior.
But please don't let my good friends be annoyed
(among whom I certainly count you, Cassius),
45   nor interpret my neglectful manner to mean any more
than that poor Brutus, at war with himself,
forgets how to show his love to other men.

CASSIUS
    Then, Brutus, I have much mistaken your troubles,
and because of that error I have kept to myself
50   very significant thoughts and my own worthy speculations.
Tell me, good Brutus, can you see your own face?

BRUTUS
    No, Cassius,
because the eye can only see itself by reflection,
by its own image in something else.

CASSIUS
    That's right.
55   And it is too bad, Brutus,
that you have no such mirrors that will reflect
your hidden worthiness into your own eyes,
that you might see your image. I have heard
that many of the most respected men in Rome—
60   except immortal Caesar—when speaking of Brutus,
and groaning under the oppression of this age,
have wished that noble Brutus had eyes in his head.

BRUTUS
    What dangers are you leading me into, Cassius,
that you want to make me look into myself
65   for something that isn't there?

CASSIUS
    Therefore, good Brutus, get ready to hear me.
And since you know that you cannot see yourself
so well as by your reflection in others, I, your mirror,
will frankly reveal to you
70   that aspect of your character that you are not yet aware of.
And don't suspect me, noble Brutus.

Were I a common laughter, or did use
To stale with ordinary oaths my love
To every new protester; if you know
75   That I do fawn on men and hug them hard,
And after scandal them; or if you know
That I profess myself in banqueting
To all the rout, then hold me dangerous.
          Flourish and shout.
BRUTUS
What means this shouting?
80   I do fear the people choose Caesar
For their king.
CASSIUS
                    Ay, do you fear it?
Then must I think you would not have it so.
BRUTUS
I would not, Cassius, yet I love him well.
But wherefore do you hold me here so long?
85   What is it that you would impart to me?
If it be aught toward the general good,
Set honor in one eye and death i' th' other,
And I will look on both indifferently;
For let the gods so speed me as I love
90   The name of honor more than I fear death.
CASSIUS
I know that virtue to be in you, Brutus,
As well as I do know your outward favor.
Well, honor is the subject of my story.
I cannot tell what you and other men
95   Think of this life; but for my single self,
I had as lief not be as live to be
In awe of such a thing as I myself.
I was born free as Caesar, so were you;
We both have fed as well, and we can both
100   Endure the winter's cold as well as he.
For once, upon a raw and gusty day,
The troubled Tiber chafing with her shores,
Caesar said to me, "Dar'st thou, Cassius, now

If I were an ordinary fool, or were accustomed,
with a drunkard's tearful vows, to reciprocate affection
with everyone who professes love for me; if you know
75   that I shamelessly flatter men and pretend to love them,
then afterwards slander them; or if you know
that, while banqueting, I promise friendship
to everyone indiscriminately—then consider me dangerous.
        Trumpet fanfare and shout off-stage.

BRUTUS
        What does this shouting mean?
80   I fear that the people choose Caesar
        for their king.

CASSIUS
        Yes, do you fear it?
        Then I must think that you don't want it to happen.

BRUTUS
        I don't Cassius, yet I love Caesar very much.
        But why do you keep me here so long?
85   What do you want to tell me?
        If it is anything for the good of the people,
        put honor in one eye and death in the other,
        and I will dare to look on both with equal courage.
        For as the gods may favor me, I love
90   the name of honor more than I fear death.

CASSIUS
        I know you have that virtue, Brutus,
        as well as I know your outward appearance.
        Well, honor is the theme of my story.
        I don't know what you and other men
95   may think of this life, but as for me,
        I would just as soon not be alive as live to be
        afraid of another man no better than myself.
        I was born as free as Caesar and so were you.
        We both have eaten as well, and we can both
100   suffer the winter's cold as well as Caesar.
        Once, on a raw and windy day,
        when the swollen Tiber was beating against its shores,
        Caesar said to me, "Do you now dare, Cassius,

Leap in with me into this angry flood,
105   And swim to yonder point?" Upon the word,
Accoutred as I was, I plungèd in
And bade him follow. So indeed he did.
The torrent roared, and we did buffet it
With lusty sinews, throwing it aside
110   And stemming it with hearts of controversy.
But ere we could arrive the point proposed,
Caesar cried, "Help me, Cassius, or I sink."
I, as Aeneas* our great ancestor
Did from the flames of Troy upon his shoulder
115   The old Anchises bear, so from the waves of Tiber
Did I the tired Caesar. And this man
Is now become a god, and Cassius is
A wretched creature, and must bend his body
If Caesar carelessly but nod on him.
120   He had a fever when he was in Spain,
And when the fit was on him, I did mark
How he did shake. 'Tis true, this god did shake.
His coward lips did from their color fly,
And that same eye, whose bend doth awe the world,
125   Did lose his luster. I did hear him groan.
Ay, and that tongue of his that bade the Romans
Mark him, and write his speeches in their books,
"Alas!" it cried, "Give me some drink, Titinius,"
As a sick girl. Ye gods, it doth amaze me
130   A man of such a feeble temper should
So get the start of the majestic world,
And bear the palm alone.
        Shout. Flourish.

BRUTUS
Another general shout?
I do believe that these applauses are
135   For some new honors that are heaped on Caesar.

CASSIUS
Why, man, he doth bestride the narrow world
Like a Colossus,* and we petty men

---

113 *Aeneas* legendary founder of the Roman state and hero of Vergil's *Aeneid.*

to leap with me into this angry river
and swim to that point over there?" As soon as I heard
105   the challenge,
dressed as I was, I plunged right in
and asked him to follow. So indeed he did.
The river roared, and we struggled against it
with all the strength we could muster, swimming against
the current
110   and working our way through it in a competitive spirit.
But before we could reach the appointed place,
Caesar cried out, "Help me, Cassius, or I'll sink."
I, like Aeneas our great ancestor (who
bore his old father Anchises on his shoulders
115   from the flames of burning Troy), carried the tired Caesar
from the waves of the Tiber. And this man
has now become a god! And Cassius is
a lowly creature and must bow in respect
even if Caesar only carelessly glances at him.
120   Caesar had a fever when he was in Spain,
and when his temperature mounted, I saw
how he shook. It's true, this god shook.
His cowardly lips grew pale,
and that same eye, whose mere glance keeps the world in awe,
125   ·became dull and lost its brightness. I heard him groan.
Yes, and·that tongue of his that commanded the Roman people
to pay attention to him and to write his speeches in their books,
"Alas!" it cried, like a sick girl, "Give me something
to drink, Titinius."
O you gods, it amazes me
130   that a man of such weak character should
surpass the rest of this glorious world
and alone reap the rewards of victory.
Shout. Trumpet flourish.

BRUTUS
Another shout from the people?
I believe that this applause is
135   for some new honors that are heaped on Caesar.

CASSIUS
Why, man, he spans this narrow world
like the Colossus, and we puny men

---

137 *Colossus* a bronze statue of Apollo as the sun god, more than 100
feet high, whose legs are said to have spanned the harbor of Rhodes.

Walk under his huge legs, and peep about
To find ourselves dishonorable graves.
140   Men at some time are masters of their fates.
The fault, dear Brutus, is not in our stars,*
But in ourselves, that we are underlings.
"Brutus" and "Caesar." What should be in that "Caesar"?
Why should that name be sounded more than yours?
145   Write them together: yours is as fair a name.
Sound them: it doth become the mouth as well.
Weigh them: it is as heavy. Conjure with 'em:
"Brutus" will start a spirit as soon as "Caesar."
Now in the names of all the gods at once,
150   Upon what meat doth this our Caesar feed
That he is grown so great? Age, thou art shamed.
Rome, thou hast lost the breed of noble bloods.
When went there by an age, since the great flood,*
But it was famed with more than with one man?
155   When could they say, till now, that talked of Rome,
That her wide walks encompassed but one man?
Now it is Rome* indeed, and room enough,
When there is in it but one only man.
O, you and I have heard our fathers say
160   There was a Brutus* once that would have brooked
Th' eternal devil to keep his state in Rome
As easily as a king.

BRUTUS
That you do love me, I am nothing jealous;
What you would work me to, I have some aim;
165   How I have thought of this, and of these times,
I shall recount hereafter. For this present,
I would not so—with love I might entreat you—
Be any further moved. What you have said,
I will consider; what you have to say,
170   I will with patience hear, and find a time
Both meet to hear and answer such high things.
Till then, my noble friend, chew upon this:
Brutus had rather be a villager

---

141 *stars* according to widely held astrological beliefs, the position of
the stars (used generally for any heavenly body) governed, or at least reflected, the affairs of men.
153 *the great flood* an early, mythical flood, in which Zeus destroyed all
of corrupt mankind except Deucalion and his wife Pyrrha.

walk under his huge legs and look timidly about
to find us dishonorable graves.

140 Men at certain times can be masters of their fates.
The trouble, dear Brutus, is not caused by the harmful influence
    of our stars,
but it's our own fault that we remain hangers-on.
Consider those names: "Brutus" and "Caesar." What is there
    special about the name "Caesar"?
Why should that name be spoken more than yours is?

145 Write them together: yours is as fine a name.
Speak them: yours sounds just as good.
Weigh them: yours is as impressive. Do magic with them:
"Brutus" will call up a spirit just as soon as "Caesar."
Now I appeal to all the gods at once to tell me

150 what food our Caesar feeds on
that he has become so great? What a shame for this age
    we live in!
Rome, you have lost the ability to breed noble heroes.
When was there ever an age, since the Great Flood,
that was not famous for more than one single man?

155 When, until now, could those who spoke of Rome say
that her wide streets contained only one man worth mentioning?
Now is it Rome indeed, and room enough,
when the whole city has only one man in it.
O, you and I have heard our fathers say

160 there was a Brutus once who would just as easily have allowed
the eternal devil to rule Rome
as a king.

BRUTUS
That you love me, I don't at all doubt.
What you would make me do, I have some idea.
How I have thought about this matter and of the times

165   in which we live,
I shall tell you about later. For the moment,
I would not—with love I beg of you—
be led any further. What you have said,
I will think over. What you have to say,

170 I will listen to patiently and find an appropriate time
to hear and to answer such important questions.
Until then, my noble friend, think about this:
Brutus would rather be a humble village-dweller

---

157 *Rome* in Shakespeare's time, "Rome" and "room" were pronounced
alike.

160 *Brutus* Lucius Junius Brutus, who drove the Tarquins out of Rome
and established the Roman Republic in 509 B.C. Marcus Brutus claimed to
be descended from him.

Than to repute himself a son of Rome
175   Under these hard conditions as this time
Is like to lay upon us.

CASSIUS
I am glad that my weak words
Have struck but thus much show of fire from Brutus.

Enter CAESAR *and his train.*

BRUTUS
The games are done, and Caesar is returning.

CASSIUS
180   As they pass by, pluck Casca by the sleeve,
And he will, after his sour fashion, tell you
What hath proceeded worthy note today.

BRUTUS
I will do so. But look you, Cassius,
The angry spot doth glow on Caesar's brow,
185   And all the rest look like a chidden train.
Calphurnia's cheek is pale, and Cicero
Looks with such ferret and such fiery eyes
As we have seen him in the Capitol,
Being crossed in conference by some senators.

CASSIUS
190   Casca will tell us what the matter is.

CAESAR
Antonio.

ANTONY
Caesar.

CAESAR
Let me have men about me that are fat,
Sleek-headed men, and such as sleep a-nights.
195   Yond Cassius has a lean and hungry look;
He thinks too much. Such men are dangerous.

ANTONY
Fear him not, Caesar, he's not dangerous.
He is a noble Roman, and well given.

CAESAR
Would he were fatter! But I fear him not.
200   Yet if my name were liable to fear,
I do not know the man I should avoid

than think of himself as a citizen of Rome
175   at this moment, when heavy burdens
are likely to be laid on us.

CASSIUS
I am glad that my weak words
have, like the flint, struck so much fire from Brutus.
       Enter CAESAR *and his followers.*

BRUTUS
The games are over, and Caesar is returning.

CASSIUS
180   As they pass by, take Casca aside,
and, in his own sour way, he will tell you
what important events happened today.

BRUTUS
I will do so. But look, Cassius,
an angry spot is glowing on Caesar's brow,
185   and all his followers look as if they've just been scolded.
Calphurnia's cheeks are pale, and Cicero,
with his little, red, fiery eyes, looks like a ferret,
just as we've seen him in the Capitol,
when some senators have disagreed with him in debate.

CASSIUS
190   Casca will tell us what's the matter.

CAESAR
Antonio.

ANTONY
Caesar.

CAESAR
I should be surrounded by fat men,
well-groomed fellows that sleep well at night.
195   Cassius over there is too lean and hungry looking;
he thinks too much. Such men are dangerous.

ANTONY
Don't fear him, Caesar, he's not dangerous.
He is a noble Roman and friendly to you.

CAESAR
I wish he were fatter! But I don't fear him.
200   Yet if the name of "Caesar" could fear anyone at all,
I do not know the man I should avoid

So soon as that spare Cassius. He reads much,
He is a great observer, and he looks
Quite through the deeds of men. He loves no plays,
205   As thou dost, Antony; he hears no music.
Seldom he smiles, and smiles in such a sort
As if he mocked himself, and scorned his spirit
That could be moved to smile at anything.
Such men as he be never at heart's ease
210   Whiles they behold a greater than themselves,
And therefore are they very dangerous.
I rather tell thee what is to be feared
That what I fear; for always I am Caesar.
Come on my right hand, for this ear is deaf,
215   And tell me truly what thou think'st of him.

Sennet. Exeunt CAESAR *and his train.*

CASCA
You pulled me by the cloak; would you speak with me?

BRUTUS
Ay, Casca, tell us what hath chanced today
That Caesar looks so sad.

CASCA
Why, you were with him, were you not?

BRUTUS
220   I should not then ask Casca what had chanced.

CASCA
Why, there was a crown offered him; and being offered him, he
put it by with the back of his hand, thus; and then the people fell
a-shouting.

BRUTUS
What was the second noise for?

CASCA
225   Why, for that too.

CASSIUS
They shouted thrice. What was the last cry for?

CASCA
Why, for that too.

BRUTUS
Was the crown offered him thrice?

so eagerly as that lean Cassius. He reads much,
he is a keen observer of human nature, and he is able to see
right through men's actions. He doesn't like plays,
205   as you do, Antony; he doesn't listen to music.
He seldom smiles, and then he smiles in such a way
as if he were mocking himself and scorning that he should
    be so weak
as to be tempted to smile at anything.
Men like him are never contented
210   while they see someone greater than themselves,
and therefore they are very dangerous.
I'm telling you what might be feared rather than
what I actually fear, since I am always Caesar
    (and therefore without fear).
Come on my right side, because my left ear is deaf,
215   and tell me what you really think of Cassius.

       Trumpet flourish. Exit CAESAR *and his followers.*

CASCA
You pulled me by my cloak. Do you want to speak with me?
BRUTUS
Yes, Casca, tell us what happened today
that makes Caesar look so serious.
CASCA
Why, you were with him, weren't you?
BRUTUS
220   If I were, then I wouldn't be asking Casca what happened.
CASCA
Why, a crown was offered him, and when it was offered, he
pushed it away with the back of his hand, like this (*making a
    disdainful gesture of refusal*). And then the people
started to shout.
BRUTUS
What was the second noise for?
CASCA
225   Why, for the same reason.
CASSIUS
The people shouted three times. What was the last cry for?
CASCA
Why, for the same reason.
BRUTUS
Was the crown offered him three times?

CASCA

230   Ay, marry, was't, and he put it by thrice, every time gentler than other; and at every putting-by mine honest neighbors shouted

CASSIUS

Who offered him the crown?

CASCA

Why, Antony.

BRUTUS

Tell us the manner of it, gentle Casca.

CASCA

I can as well be hanged as tell the manner of it: it was mere
235   foolery; I did not mark it. I saw Mark Antony offer him a crown
—yet 'twas not a crown neither, 'twas one of these coronets—
and, as I told you, he put it by once; but for all that, to my
thinking, he would fain have had it. Then he offered it to him
again; then he put it by again; but to my thinking, he was very
240   loath to lay his fingers off it. And then he offered it the third
time. He put it the third time by; and still as he refused it, the
rabblement hooted, and clapped their chopt hands, and threw
up their sweaty nightcaps, and uttered such a deal of stinking
breath because Caesar refused the crown, that it had, almost,
245   choked Caesar; for he swounded and fell down at it. And for
mine own part, I durst not laugh, for fear of opening my lips
and receiving the bad air.

CASSIUS

But soft, I pray you. What, did Caesar swound?

CASCA

He fell down in the market place and foamed at mouth and was
250   speechless.

BRUTUS

'Tis very like he hath the falling sickness.*

---

251   *falling sickness* epilepsy. In the next lines Cassius turns "falling sickness" into a political metaphor for willing subjection.

CASCA

Yes indeed it was, and he refused it three times,
each time more reluctantly than
230 the other. And at each refusal the worthy Roman mob shouted.

CASSIUS

Who offered him the crown?

CASCA

Why, Antony.

BRUTUS

Tell us how it happened, gentle Casca.

CASCA

I can just as easily be hanged as tell how it happened.
The whole affair seemed like
foolishness but was actually a set-up—I didn't pay attention
235 to it. I saw Mark Antony offer Caesar a crown—
yet it wasn't really a crown, but more like a little coronet—
and, as I told you, Caesar refused it once. But, despite that, I
think he would have taken it gladly. Then Antony
offered it to him
again. Then Caesar refused it again, but, in my opinion,
he was very
hesitant to take his fingers off it. And then Antony offered
240 it the third
time. Caesar refused it for the third time. And all the while
he refused it,
the rabble hooted and clapped their rough hands, and threw
their sweaty nightcaps up in the air, and exhaled
so much stinking
breath because Caesar refused the crown that it almost
choked Caesar, because he fainted and fell down on
45 the ground. As for
me, I didn't dare to laugh for fear of opening my lips
and breathing in the bad air.

CASSIUS

But wait a minute, I beg you. What, did Caesar faint?

CASCA

He fell down in the market place and foamed at the mouth and
50 couldn't speak.

BRUTUS

It's very likely that he has epilepsy.

CASSIUS

No, Caesar hath it not; but you, and I,
And honest Casca, we have the falling sickness.

CASCA

255
I know not what you mean by that, but I am sure Caesar fell
down. If the tag-rag people did not clap him and hiss him,
according as he pleased and displeased them, as they use to do
the players in the theater, I am no true man.

BRUTUS

What said he when he came unto himself?

CASCA

260
Marry, before he fell down, when he perceived the common
herd was glad he refused the crown, he plucked me ope his
doublet and offered them his throat to cut. And I had been a
man of any occupation, if I would not have taken him at a
word, I would I might go to hell among the rogues. And so he
fell. When he came to himself again, he said, if he had done or
265
said anything amiss, he desired their worships to think it was
his infirmity. Three or four wenches where I stood cried, "Alas,
good soul!" and forgave him with all their hearts. But there's
no heed to be taken of them; if Caesar had stabbed their mothers,
they would have done no less.

BRUTUS

270
And after that, he came thus sad away?

CASCA

Ay.

CASSIUS

Did Cicero say anything?

CASCA

Ay, he spoke Greek.

CASSIUS

To what effect?

CASCA

275
Nay, and I tell you that, I'll ne'er look you i' th' face again. But
those that understood him smiled at one another and shook

CASSIUS

 No, Caesar doesn't have it, but you and I

 and honest Casca, we have the "falling sickness."

CASCA

255 I don't know what you mean by that, but I am sure Caesar fell

 down. If the ragged mob didn't clap him and hiss him

 as his performance pleased or displeased them—

  which they usually do with

 actors in the theater—I am not an honest man.

BRUTUS

 What did Caesar say when he came to?

CASCA

 Well, before he fell down, when he saw that the

260 mob was glad he refused the crown, he opened his

 jacket and offered to let them cut his throat. If I had been a

 more industrious man, I would have taken him at

 his word, or may I go to hell with other villains. And then he

 fell down. When he came to again, he said that if he had done or

 said anything wrong, he assured the worthy people it was

265 because of

 his illness. Three or four girls near where I stood

  cried out "Alas,

 good soul!" and forgave him with all their hearts.

  But one shouldn't pay

 much attention to them: if Caesar had stabbed their mothers,

 they would have had the same response.

BRUTUS

270 And after that he left the market place with such a serious look?

CASCA

 Yes.

CASSIUS

 Did Cicero say anything?

CASCA

 Yes, he spoke Greek.

CASSIUS

 What did he say?

CASCA

 No, if I tell you that, I'll never be able to look you square

275 in the eye again. But

 those that understood him smiled knowingly at

  one another and shook

their heads; but for mine own part, it was Greek to me. I could tell you more news too. Murellus and Flavius, for pulling scarfs off Caesar's images, are put to silence. Fare you well. There was 280 more foolery yet, if I could remember it.

CASSIUS
Will you sup with me tonight, Casca?

CASCA
No, I am promised forth.

CASSIUS
Will you dine with me tomorrow?

CASCA
Ay, if I be alive, and your mind hold, and your dinner worth 285 the eating.

CASSIUS
Good; I will expect you.

CASCA
Do so. Farewell both.
    Exit.

BRUTUS
What a blunt fellow is this grown to be!
He was quick mettle when he went to school.

CASSIUS
290 So is he now, in execution
Of any bold or noble enterprise,
However he puts on this tardy form.
This rudeness is a sauce to his good wit,
Which gives men stomach to disgest his words
295 With better appetite.

BRUTUS
And so it is. For this time I will leave you.
Tomorrow, if you please to speak with me,
I will come home to you; or if you will,
Come home to me, and I will wait for you.

CASSIUS
300 I will do so. Till then, think of the world.
    Exit BRUTUS.

their heads; but, to tell you the truth, it was Greek
    to me. I could
tell you more news too. Murellus and Flavius, arrested for
    stripping the victory ornaments
off Caesar's statues, have been forced to keep quiet.
    Farewell, Cassius. There was
280   still more fooling around, if I could only remember it.

CASSIUS
Will you have dinner with me tonight, Casca?

CASCA
No, I've already promised someone else.

CASSIUS
Will you dine with me tomorrow?

CASCA
Yes, if I'm still alive, and you don't change your mind,
    and your dinner is worth
285   eating.

CASSIUS
Good. I will expect you.

CASCA
Do that. Farewell to both of you.
    Exit.

BRUTUS
How slow and dull Casca has become!
He was much livelier when he went to school.

CASSIUS
290   He still is, in doing
any bold or noble enterprise,
regardless of how he pretends to be slow and stupid.
This coarseness is a spice to make his intelligence
    more appetizing,
and to tempt men to listen to him
295   with a keener appetite.

BRUTUS
That may be true. I must leave you now.
Tomorrow, if you wish to speak with me,
I will come to your house. Or, if you prefer,
come to my house, and I will wait for you.

CASSIUS
I will do so. Until then, think about the political situation
300   in Rome.
    Exit BRUTUS.

Well, Brutus, thou art noble; yet I see
Thy honorable mettle may be wrought
From that it is disposed. Therefore it is meet
That noble minds keep ever with their likes;
305   For who so firm that cannot be seduced?
Caesar doth bear me hard, but he loves Brutus.
If I were Brutus now and he were Cassius,
He should not humor me. I will this night,
In several hands, in at his windows throw,
310   As if they came from several citizens,
Writings, all tending to the great opinion
That Rome holds of his name; wherein obscurely
Caesar's ambition shall be glancèd at.
And after this, let Caesar seat him sure,
315   For we shall shake him, or worse days endure.
        Exit.

[*Scene iii: Rome, a street.*] *Thunder and lightning. Enter* CASCA
and CICERO [*at different doors*].

CICERO
Good even, Casca. Brought you Caesar home?
Why are you breathless, and why stare you so?

CASCA
Are not you moved, when all the sway of earth
Shakes like a thing unfirm? O Cicero,
5   I have seen tempests, when the scolding winds
Have rived the knotty oaks, and I have seen
Th' ambitious ocean swell and rage and foam,
To be exalted with the threat'ning clouds;
But never till tonight, never till now,
10   Did I go through a tempest dropping fire.
Either there is a civil strife in heaven,
Or else the world, too saucy with the gods,
Incenses them to send destruction.

CICERO
Why, saw you anything more wonderful?

(*To himself*) Well, Brutus, I admit that you are noble.
   Yet I also see that
your honorable nature can be twisted
from its true inclinations. Therefore, it is proper that
high-minded people should deal only with others like themselves.

305   For what man is so strong-willed that he can't be won over?
Caesar is against me, but he loves Brutus.
If I were Brutus now and Brutus were Cassius,
I would not let him persuade me the way I've done him. Tonight,
I'll forge some letters in different handwritings and throw them
    into Brutus's windows,

310   as if they came from various Roman citizens,
all harping on the high respect
in which Brutus is held in Rome; but secretly
Caesar's ambition shall also be hinted at.
Now that we have begun our plot, let Caesar make sure
    of his position,
because we're going to shake him out of his imagined throne, or

315   suffer the consequences.
    Exit.

Scene iii: A street in Rome. Thunder and lightning. Enter CASCA
and CICERO *from separate entrances.*

CICERO
Good evening, Casca. Did you bring Caesar home?
Why are you breathless, and why do you stare?
CASCA
Aren't you disturbed when the whole earth
shakes like something sick? O Cicero,

5   I have seen storms, when winds sent to punish the earth
have split knotty oak trees, and I have seen
ocean waves swell and rage and foam, ambitious
to reach the very clouds that threatened them.
But never until tonight, never until now,

10   did I experience a storm that dropped fire on the earth.
Either there is a civil war in heaven,
or else the world, too insolent with the gods,
angers them to destroy the earth.
CICERO
Why, did you see anything more remarkable than what
    you've described?

CASCA

15   A common slave—you know him well by sight—
Held up his left hand, which did flame and burn
Like twenty torches joined; and yet his hand,
Not sensible of fire, remained unscorched.
Besides—I ha' not since put up my sword—
20   Against the Capitol I met a lion,
Who glazed upon me, and went surly by
Without annoying me. And there were drawn
Upon a heap a hundred ghastly women,
Transformèd with their fear, who swore they saw
25   Men, all in fire, walk up and down the streets.
And yesterday the bird of night did sit,
Even at noonday, upon the market place,
Hooting and shrieking. When these prodigies
Do so conjointly meet, let not men say,
30   "These are their reasons, they are natural,"
For I believe they are portentous things
Unto the climate that they point upon.

CICERO

    Indeed, it is a strange-disposèd time.
But men may construe things after their fashion,
35   Clean from the purpose of the things themselves.
Comes Caesar to the Capitol tomorrow?

CASCA

    He doth; for he did bid Antonio
Send word to you he would be there tomorrow.

CICERO

    Good night then, Casca.
40   This disturbèd sky is not to walk in.

CASCA

    Farewell, Cicero.
        Exit CICERO.
        Enter CASSIUS.

CASCA

15 An ordinary slave—you know him well by sight—
held up his left hand, which flamed and burned
like twenty torches joined together, and yet his hand,
not feeling the fire, remained unscorched.
Besides—I haven't sheathed my sword since then—
20 I met a lion opposite the Capitol building,
which stared at me and then passed by sullenly
without doing any harm. And there was a
crowd of a hundred terrified women
transformed with their fear, who swore they saw
25 men in flames walking up and down the streets.
And yesterday a screech owl sat
even at noon in the market place,
hooting and shrieking. When these unnatural wonders
all occur together, don't let men say,
30 "Such and such are the reasons, they are natural occurrences,"
because I believe that they are completely strange events,
    full of meaning
for the place where they occur.

CICERO

Indeed, these times are abnormal.
But men may interpret things any way they please,
35 and sometimes just the opposite of their actual meaning.
Is Caesar coming to the Capitol tomorrow?

CASCA

He is, because he told Antonio
to let you know that he would be there tomorrow.

CICERO

Good night then, Casca.
40 When the sky is so stormy, it's not a good idea to walk around.

CASCA

Farewell, Cicero.
    Exit CICERO.
    Enter CASSIUS.

CASSIUS
  Who's there?
CASCA
                    A Roman.
CASSIUS
                              Casca, by your voice.
CASCA
  Your ear is good. Cassius, what night is this!
CASSIUS
  A very pleasing night to honest men.
CASCA
45 Who ever knew the heavens menace so?
CASSIUS
  Those that have known the earth so full of faults.
  For my part, I have walked about the streets,
  Submitting me unto the perilous night,
  And thus unbracèd, Casca, as you see,
50 Have bared my bosom to the thunder-stone;
  And when the cross blue lightning seemed to open
  The breast of heaven, I did present myself
  Even in the aim and very flash of it.
CASCA
  But wherefore did you so much tempt the heavens?
55 It is the part of men to fear and tremble
  When the most mighty gods by tokens send
  Such dreadful heralds to astonish us.
CASSIUS
  You are dull, Casca,
  And those sparks of life that should be in a Roman
60 You do want, or else you use not.
  You look pale, and gaze, and put on fear,
  And cast yourself in wonder,
  To see the strange impatience of the heavens,
  But if you would consider the true cause—
65 Why all these fires; why all these gliding ghosts;
  Why birds and beasts, from quality and kind;
  Why old men, fools, and children calculate;
  Why all these things change from their ordinance,
  Their natures, and preformèd faculties,

CASSIUS
  Who's there?

CASCA
  A Roman.

CASSIUS
  It's Casca! I recognize your voice.

CASCA
  You have a good ear. Cassius, what a night this is!

CASSIUS
  It's a very pleasing night to honest men.

CASCA
45 Who ever knew the heavens to be so threatening?

CASSIUS
  Those who have known the earth to be so full of crimes.
  As for me, I have walked about the streets,
  eagerly experiencing this stormy and dangerous night,
  and thus, with unbuttoned jacket, Casca, as you can see,
50 I have exposed my naked chest to the thunder-bolt.
  And when the forked blue lightning seemed to show
  the breast of heaven, I presented myself
  as a target for the flashes to aim at.

CASCA
  But why did you tempt the heavens so much?
55 Men are supposed to be afraid and tremble
  when the most mighty gods send
  such fearful signs as their messengers to astonish us.

CASSIUS
  You are dull, Casca,
  and either you lack the wit a Roman should have,
60 or else you don't know how to use it.
  You look pale, and gaze, and show fear,
  and throw yourself into a state of amazement,
  because you see the strange passion of the heavens.
  But if you would consider the true cause—
  why all these fires; why all these ghosts gliding about;
  why birds and beasts are acting so contrary to their nature;
  why even old men, fools, and children are able to understand the
    signs of the heavens and prophesy from them;
  why all these things turn away from their established order,
  their natures and inherent qualities,

70   To monstrous quality—why, you shall find
        That heaven hath infused them with these spirits
        To make them instruments of fear and warning
        Unto some monstrous state.
        Now could I, Casa, name to thee a man
75   Most like this dreadful night,
        That thunders, lightens, opens graves, and roars
        As doth the lion in the Capitol;
        A man no mightier than thyself or me
        In personal action, yet prodigious grown,
80   And fearful, as these strange eruptions are.

CASCA
        'Tis Caesar that you mean, is it not, Cassius?

CASSIUS
        Let it be who it is; for Romans now
        Have thews and limbs like to their ancestors.
        But woe the while! Our fathers' minds are dead,
85   And we are governed with our mothers' spirits;
        Our yoke and sufferance show us womanish.

CASCA
        Indeed, they say the senators tomorrow
        Mean to establish Caesar as a king;
        And he shall wear his crown by sea and land
90   In every place, save here in Italy.

CASSIUS
        I know where I will wear this dagger then;
        Cassius from bondage will deliver Cassius.
        Therein, ye gods, you make the weak most strong;
        Therein, ye gods, you tyrants do defeat.
95   Nor stony tower, nor walls of beaten brass,
        Nor airless dungeon, nor strong links of iron,
        Can be retentive to the strength of spirit;
        But life, being weary of these worldly bars,
        Never lacks power to dismiss itself.

and are transformed into something monstrous—
70   why, you shall find
that heaven has endowed these things with a special power
to make them signs of fear and warning
to a nation that has become monstrous.
I could now, Casca, name a man
75   who is most like this fearful night,
a man who thunders, lightens, opens graves, and roars
like the lion in the Capitol.
He is a man no mightier than you or I
in his personal life, but in public he has grown into
          something ominous
80   and fearful, as are these strange disturbances of the heaven.

CASCA
It's Caesar that you mean, is it not, Cassius?

CASSIUS
Let it be whoever it is. Romans now
are still strong and powerfully built like their ancestors.
But what a terrible tragedy! The manliness of our fathers
          is dead,
85   and we are ruled by the weak, feminine spirits of our mothers.
To let ourselves willingly be subdued and put up with wrongs
          shows that we are womanish.

CASCA
Indeed, they say the senators tomorrow
intend to make Caesar king,
and he will be permitted to wear his crown on sea and land
90   everywhere, except here in Italy.

CASSIUS
I know where I will wear this dagger then;
Cassius will free himself from slavery.
In that way, you gods, you make weak men very strong;
in that way, you gods, you make it possible to defeat tyrants.
95   Not a stone tower, nor walls of beaten brass,
nor a suffocating dungeon, nor the strong links of an iron chain
are powerful enough against the strength of a courageous spirit.
But life, weary of being imprisoned in this world,
never lacks the power to end its existence.

100   If I know this, know all the world besides,
       That part of tyranny that I do bear
       I can shake off at pleasure.
               Thunder still.

CASCA
                              So can I.
       So every bondman in his own hand bears
       The power to cancel his captivity.

CASSIUS
105   And why should Caesar be a tyrant then?
       Poor man, I know he would not be a wolf
       But that he sees the Romans are but sheep;
       He were no lion, were not Romans hinds.
       Those that with haste will make a mighty fire
110   Begin it with weak straws. What trash is Rome,
       What rubbish and what offal, when it serves
       For the base matter to illuminate
       So vile a thing as Caesar! But, O grief,
       Where hast thou led me? I, perhaps, speak this
115   Before a willing bondman; then I know
       My answer must be made. But I am armed,
       And dangers are to me indifferent.

CASCA
       You speak to Casca, and to such a man
       That is no fleering telltale. Hold, my hand.
120   Be factious for redress of all these griefs,
       And I will set this foot of mine as far
       As who goes farthest.

CASSIUS
                       There's a bargain made.
       Now know you, Casca, I have moved already
       Some certain of the noblest-minded Romans
125   To undergo with me an enterprise
       Of honorable-dangerous consequence;
       And I do know by this, they stay for me
       In Pompey's porch;* for now, this fearful night,
       There is no stir or walking in the streets,

---

128 *Pompey's porch* the portico or colonnade of the theater built by
Pompey in the Campus Martius in 55 B.C. Caesar's murder, which in Plutarch

100 If I am sure of this let all the world know too:
that portion of tyranny that I endure
I can throw off whenever I want to (i.e., by killing myself).
It continues to thunder.

CASCA
So can I.
So every slave has in his own hands
the power to end his captivity.

CASSIUS
105 Then why should Caesar be a tyrant?
Poor man, I know he would not be a wolf
if he didn't see that the Roman people are sheep.
He wouldn't be a lion if the Romans didn't show themselves
to be deer.
People who want to make a big fire quickly
110 start it with little bits of straw. What mere kindling is Rome,
what rubbish and what stinking guts, when it lets itself be used
as the worthless stuff to light up
so vile a thing as Caesar! But, O my grief,
where have you led me? Perhaps I am now speaking this
115 before a willing slave; then I know
what answer I must make for myself. But I am armed,
and dangers don't matter to me.

CASCA
You are speaking to Casca, and to the kind of man
that is no sneering tattle-tale. Wait a minute, here's my hand.
120 Let's join together to set right all of our grievances,
and I will go as far
as whoever goes furthest.

CASSIUS
That's a deal.
Now let me inform you, Casca, that I have already persuaded
some of the noblest-minded Romans
125 to undertake an action with me
that will have results both honorable and dangerous.
I'm sure that by this time, they are waiting for me
in Pompey's portico. Right now, in this fear-provoking night,
nothing is stirring and nobody is walking in the streets,

---

takes place in Pompey's porch, is transferred by Shakespeare to the Capitol,
by which he means the Senate House, a building also erected by Pompey.

130   And the complexion of the element
         In favor's like the work we have in hand,
         Most bloody, fiery, and most terrible.
                Enter CINNA.
CASCA
         Stand close awhile, for here comes one in haste.
CASSIUS
         'Tis Cinna; I do know him by his gait.
135   He is a friend. Cinna, where haste you so?
CINNA
         To find out you. Who's that, Metellus Cimber?
CASSIUS
         No, it is Casca, one incorporate
         To our attempts. Am I not stayed for, Cinna?
CINNA
         I am glad on't. What a fearful night is this!
140   There's two or three of us have seen strange sights.
CASSIUS
         Am I not stayed for? Tell me.
CINNA
                              Yes, you are. O Cassius,
         If you could but win the noble Brutus
         To our party—
CASSIUS
         Be you content. Good Cinna, take this paper,
145   And look you lay it in the praetor's chair,
         Where Brutus may but find it; and throw this
         In at his window; set this up with wax
         Upon old Brutus'* statue. All this done,
         Repair to Pompey's porch, where you shall find us.
150   Is Decius Brutus and Trebonius there?
CINNA
         All but Metellus Cimber, and he's gone
         To seek you at your house. Well, I will hie,
         And so bestow these papers as you bade me.
CASSIUS
         That done, repair to Pompey's theater.*
                Exit CINNA.

---

148 *old Brutus'*   Lucius Junius Brutus'. See note at 1.2.160.

130   and the appearance of the sky
is like the task we are now undertaking:
most bloody, fiery, and most terrible.
    Enter CINNA.

CASCA
Stand aside for a while, because here comes someone in haste.

CASSIUS
It's Cinna; I know him by his walk.
135   He is a friend. Cinna, where are you going in such a hurry?

CINNA
To find you. Who's that, Metellus Cimber?

CASSIUS
No, it is Casca, someone who's in
on our plot. Aren't they waiting for me, Cinna?

CINNA
I'm glad about that. What a fearful night this is!
140   Two or three of us have seen strange sights.

CASSIUS
Aren't they waiting for me? Tell me.

CINNA
Yes, they are. O Cassius,
if you could only win over the noble Brutus
to our party—

CASSIUS
Don't worry about that. Good Cinna, take this note,
145   and make sure to place it on the chair of the chief magistrate,
where only Brutus may find it. And throw this letter
into his window. Attach this paper with wax
to the statue of Brutus's famous ancestor. When all this is done,
come to Pompey's portico, where you shall find us.
150   Are Decius Brutus and Trebonius there?

CINNA
All except Metellus Cimber, and he's gone
to look for you at your house. Well, I will run along
and put these papers where you asked me to.

CASSIUS
When you've done that, go to Pompey's theater.
    Exit CINNA.

---

154 *Pompey's theater*   see note at 1.3.128.

155   Come, Casca, you and I will yet, ere day,
    See Brutus at his house. Three parts of him
    Is ours already, and the man entire
    Upon the next encounter yields him ours.

CASCA
    O, he sits high in all the people's hearts;
160   And that which would appear offense in us,
    His countenance, like richest alchemy,
    Will change to virtue and to worthiness.

CASSIUS
    Him and his worth and our great need of him
    You have right well conceited. Let us go,
165   For it is after midnight, and ere day
    We will awake him and be sure of him.
        Exeunt.

Act II, [Scene i: Rome]. Enter BRUTUS *in his orchard.*

BRUTUS
    What, Lucius, ho!
    I cannot, by the progress of the stars,
    Give guess how near to day. Lucius, I say!
    I would it were my fault to sleep so soundly.
5   When, Lucius, when? Awake, I say! What, Lucius!
        Enter LUCIUS.

LUCIUS
    Called you, my lord?

BRUTUS
    Get me a taper in my study, Lucius;
    When it is lighted, come and call me here.

LUCIUS
    I will, my lord.
        Exit.

BRUTUS
10   It must be by his death; and for my part,
    I know no personal cause to spurn at him,
    But for the general: he would be crowned.
    How that might change his nature, there's the question.

155   Come, Casca, you and I will still, before daybreak,
          see Brutus at his house. Three-quarters of him
          we've already won over, and the whole man
          will yield completely to us when we next meet him.

CASCA
          O, he has a high place in the hearts of the Roman people,
160   and what would appear offensive if we did it,
          his approval, like precious alchemy,
          will transform it to something virtuous and worthy.

CASSIUS
          Brutus's value and our great need of him
          you have judged correctly. Let us go,
165   because it is now after midnight, and before daybreak
          we will awake him and make sure he is with us.
                 They exit.

Act II, Scene i: Rome. Enter BRUTUS *in his garden.*

BRUTUS (*calling his servant, who is off-stage*)
          Come here, Lucius!
          I cannot, by the movement of the stars,
          guess how close it is to daybreak. Lucius, where are you?
          I wish it were my vice to be able to sleep so soundly.
          When are you coming, Lucius, when? Wake up, I say!
5   Get moving, Lucius!
                 Enter LUCIUS.

LUCIUS
          Did you call me, my lord?

BRUTUS
          Put a candle in my study, Lucius.
          When it is lighted, come here and call me.

LUCIUS
          I will, my lord.
                 Exit.

BRUTUS
10   It has to be by Caesar's death. But as for me,
          I don't have any personal reasons to be scornful of him—
          there's only the general reason: he wants to be crowned king.
          How that event might change his nature, that's the problem.

It is the bright day that brings forth the adder,
15   And that craves wary walking. Crown him—that—
And then I grant we put a sting in him,
That at his will he may do danger with.
Th' abuse of greatness is, when it disjoins
Remorse from power. And to speak truth of Caesar,
20   I have not known when his affections swayed
More than his reason. But 'tis a common proof
That lowliness is young ambition's ladder,
Whereto the climber upward turns his face;
But when he once attains the upmost round,
25   He then unto the ladder turns his back,
Looks in the clouds, scorning the base degrees*
By which he did ascend. So Caesar may;
Then lest he may, prevent. And since the quarrel
Will bear no color for the thing he is,
30   Fashion it thus: that what he is, augmented,
Would run to these and these extremities;
And therefore think him as a serpent's egg,
Which hatched, would as his kind grow mischievous,
And kill him in the shell.
       Enter LUCIUS.

LUCIUS
35   The taper burneth in your closet, sir.
Searching the window for a flint, I found
This paper, thus sealed up, and I am sure
It did not lie there when I went to bed.
       Gives him the letter.

BRUTUS
Get you to bed again, it is not day.
40   Is not tomorrow, boy, the ides of March?*

LUCIUS
I know not, sir.

BRUTUS
Look in the calendar and bring me word.

---

26 *base degrees* Brutus is thinking about the lower public offices from
which Caesar has risen, and the base and vile public by whose favor he has

A sunny day encourages vipers to come out into the open,
and forces us to walk very cautiously. If we crown Caesar—
15   if we do that—
then I grant that we give him a fang like a snake
that he may, as he pleases, do harm with.
The fault of greatness is when it separates
pity from its own power. And to tell the truth about Caesar,
20   I have never known him to let his passions rule
over his reason. But it often happens
in the early stages of ambition that humility is a ladder,
on which the climber mounts with his face turned upward.
Once he gets to the top rung, however,
25   he turns his back to the ladder
and looks into the clouds, scorning the lowly rungs below him
by which he climbed to the top. That's what Caesar may do;
then, for fear that he may, we must prevent him. And since my
          quarrel with Caesar
cannot be justified by what he actually is,
I must work it out in this way: that what he is, developed
30   and extended,
is likely to reach such and such extremes.
And therefore I must think of him as a serpent's egg,
which, once it is hatched, will grow malicious as snakes
          naturally are,
so that I must kill Caesar while he is still in the shell.
          Enter LUCIUS.

LUCIUS
35   The candle is burning in your study, sir.
Looking around the window for a piece of flint, I found
this letter, sealed up the way you see it, and I am sure
it wasn't there when I went to bed.
          Gives him the letter.

BRUTUS
Go to bed again; it isn't day yet.
40   Isn't tomorrow, boy, the ides of March?

LUCIUS
I don't know, sir.

BRUTUS
Look at the calendar and let me know.

---

been able to attain "the upmost round."
   40 *ides of March*   see note at 1.2.18.

LUCIUS
>I will, sir.
>>*Exit.*

BRUTUS
>The exhalations, whizzing in the air,
>Give so much light that I may read by them.
>>*Opens the letter and reads.*
>>"Brutus, thou sleep'st. Awake, and see thyself.
>>Shall Rome, &c. Speak, strike, redress!
>>Brutus, thou sleep'st. Awake!"
>Such instigations have been often dropped
>Where I have took them up.
>"Shall Rome, &c." Thus must I piece it out:
>Shall Rome stand under one man's awe? What, Rome?
>My ancestors did from the streets of Rome
>The Tarquin drive, when he was called a king.
>"Speak, strike, redress!" Am I entreated
>To speak and strike? O Rome, I make thee promise,
>If the redress will follow, thou receivest
>Thy full petition at the hand of Brutus.
>>*Enter* LUCIUS.

LUCIUS
>Sir, March is wasted fifteen days.
>>*Knock within.*

BRUTUS
>'Tis good. Go to the gate; somebody knocks.
>>[*Exit* LUCIUS.]
>Since Cassius first did whet me against Caesar,
>I have not slept.
>Between the acting of a dreadful thing
>And the first motion, all the interim is
>Like a phantasma or a hideous dream.
>The Genius* and the mortal instruments
>Are then in council; and the state of a man,
>Like to a little kingdom, suffers then
>The nature of an insurrection.
>>*Enter* LUCIUS.

45
50
55
60
65

---

66 *Genius* the Romans believed that each man had a guardian spirit that attended him from birth (the same as the Greek "daemon" or "demon").

LUCIUS
>I will, sir.
>>*Exit.*

BRUTUS
>The meteors, whizzing in the sky,
45
>give off so much light that I can read by them.
>>*Opens the letter and reads.*
>>"Brutus, you are asleep. Wake up and see yourself.
>>Shall Rome, etc. Speak, strike, correct wrongs!
>>Brutus, you are asleep. Wake up!"
>Such hinting letters have often been dropped
50
>where I have picked them up.
>"Shall Rome, etc." I must fill in the blanks in this way:
>Shall Rome be cowed by the rule of one single man?
>>What is Rome coming to?
>My ancestors drove the tyrant Tarquin from the streets of Rome
>when he was called a king.
55
>"Speak, strike, correct wrongs!" Am I begged
>to speak and strike? O Rome, I make you a promise,
>if good will come from my action, you will get
>everything you ask for from the hands of Brutus.
>>*Enter* LUCIUS.

LUCIUS
>Sir, fifteen days have already passed in March.
>>*Sound of knocking off-stage.*

BRUTUS
60
>That's good. Go to the gate; somebody knocks.
>>*Exit* LUCIUS.
>Since Cassius first stirred me up against Caesar,
>I have not slept.
>Between the time when we actually do something fearful
>and our first impulse to do it, all the period in between is
65
>like an hallucination or a nightmare.
>A man's guardian spirit and his physical powers
>consult with each other. And the inner state of a man,
>like the larger political state, undergoes
>its own kind of revolution (with the forces of the spirit and
>>the body pitted against each other).
>>*Enter* LUCIUS.

LUCIUS

70   Sir, 'tis your brother* Cassius at the door,
    Who doth desire to see you.

BRUTUS

                                    Is he alone?

LUCIUS

    No, sir, there are moe with him.

BRUTUS

                        Do you know them?

LUCIUS

    No, sir; their hats are plucked about their ears
    And half their faces buried in their cloaks,
75   That by no means I may discover them
    By any mark of favor.

BRUTUS

                    Let 'em enter.
        [*Exit* LUCIUS.]
    They are the faction. O Conspiracy,
    Sham'st thou to show thy dang'rous brow by night,
    When evils are most free? O then, by day
80   Where wilt thou find a cavern dark enough
    To mask thy monstrous visage? Seek none, Conspiracy;
    Hide it in smiles and affability.
    For if thou path, thy native semblance on,
    Not Erebus itself were dim enough
85   To hide thee from prevention.
            Enter the conspirators, CASSIUS, CASCA, DECIUS, CINNA,
                METELLUS, *and* TREBONIUS.

CASSIUS

    I think we are too bold upon your rest.
    Good morrow, Brutus, do we trouble you?

BRUTUS

    I have been up this hour, awake all night.
    Know I these men that come along with you?

CASSIUS

90   Yes, every man of them; and no man here
    But honors you; and every one doth wish

---

70 *brother* brother-in-law. Cassius was married to Junia, the sister of
Brutus.

LUCIUS
70   Sir, your brother-in-law Cassius is at the door,
        and he wishes to see you.

BRUTUS
        Is he alone?

LUCIUS
        No, sir, there are some other men with him.

BRUTUS
        Do you know them?

LUCIUS
        No, sir. Their hats are pulled down about their ears
        and half their faces are buried in their cloaks,
75   so that I can't recognize them
        by their features.

BRUTUS
        Let them enter.
                Exit LUCIUS.
        They are the political party (that opposes Caesar). O Conspiracy,
        are you ashamed to show your dangerous-looking face even
                at night,
        when evil things are most free to roam about? O then,
                during the day
80   where will you find a cave dark enough
        to conceal your monstrous face? Don't look for any, Conspiracy.
        Hide your face in smiles and pleasant manners,
        because if you went around showing yourself as you really are,
        hell itself wouldn't be dark enough
85   to keep you from being discovered.
                Enter the conspirators, CASSIUS, CASCA, DECIUS,
                CINNA, METELLUS, *and* TREBONIUS.

CASSIUS
        I think we are intruding too boldly on your rest.
        Good morning, Brutus. Are we disturbing you?

BRUTUS
        I just got up, but I've been awake all night.
        Do I know these men who come along with you?

CASSIUS
90   Yes, every one of them. And there is no man here
        who doesn't honor you, and every one of them wishes

You had but that opinion of yourself
Which every noble Roman bears of you.
This is Trebonius.

BRUTUS

He is welcome hither.

CASSIUS

This, Decius Brutus.

BRUTUS

95   He is welcome too.

CASSIUS

This, Casca; this, Cinna; and this, Metellus Cimber.

BRUTUS

They are all welcome.
What watchful cares do interpose themselves
Betwixt your eyes and night?

CASSIUS

100   Shall I entreat a word?

They whisper.

DECIUS

Here lies the east. Doth not the day break here?

CASCA

No.

CINNA

O pardon, sir, it doth; and yon gray lines
That fret the clouds are messengers of day.

CASCA

105   You shall confess that you are both deceived.
Here, as I point my sword, the sun arises,
Which is a great way growing on the south,
Weighing the youthful season of the year.
Some two months hence, up higher toward the north
110   He first presents his fire; and the high east
Stands as the Capitol, directly here.

BRUTUS

Give me your hands all over, one by one.

CASSIUS

And let us swear our resolution.

that you had as high an opinion of yourself
as every noble Roman has of you.
This is Trebonius.

BRUTUS
He is welcome here.

CASSIUS
This is Decius Brutus.

BRUTUS
95 He is welcome too.

CASSIUS
This, Casca; this, Cinna; and this, Metellus Cimber.

BRUTUS
They are all welcome.
What sleepless worries intrude between
your eyes and the night (and prevent you from sleeping)?

CASSIUS
100 May I have a word with you in private?
        CASSIUS *and* BRUTUS *whisper to each other.*

DECIUS
In this direction lies the east. Doesn't day break here?

CASCA
No.

CINNA
O pardon me, sir, it does, and those gray lines up there
that streak the clouds are messengers of day.

CASCA (*speaking aimlessly, as if to fill up the time*)
105 I'll make you confess that you are both wrong.
Here, in the direction I point my sword, is where the sun rises,
which is a good way toward the south,
if we consider how early in the spring it is.
Two months from now, up higher toward the north
110 is where the sun first presents its fire. And due east
is in the direction of the Capitol—right here.

BRUTUS (*addressing the conspirators*)
Give me your hands, everyone, one by one.

CASSIUS
And let us swear what we have resolved to do.

BRUTUS
No, not an oath. If not the face of men,
115 The sufferance of our souls, the time's abuse—
If these be motives weak, break off betimes,
And every man hence to his idle bed.
So let high-sighted tyranny range on
Till each man drop by lottery. But if these,
120 As I am sure they do, bear fire enough
To kindle cowards, and to steel with valor
The melting spirits of women, then, countrymen,
What need we any spur but our own cause
To prick us to redress? What other bond
125 Than secret Romans that have spoke the word
And will not palter? And what other oath
Than honesty to honesty engaged
That this shall be or we will fall for it?
Swear priests and cowards and men cautelous,
130 Old feeble carrions and such suffering souls
That welcome wrongs. Unto bad causes swear
Such creatures as men doubt; but do not stain
The even virtue of our enterprise,
Nor th' insuppressive mettle of our spirits,
135 To think that or our cause or our performance
Did need an oath; when every drop of blood
That every Roman bears, and nobly bears,
Is guilty of a several bastardy
If he do break the smallest particle
140 Of any promise that hath passed from him.

CASSIUS
But what of Cicero? Shall we sound him?
I think he will stand very strong with us.

CASCA
Let us not leave him out.

CINNA
                              No, by no means.

BRUTUS

No, not an oath. If our troubled looks,
the sufferings of our souls, the corruption of these times—
if these are weak motives for conspiracy, let us break off at once,
and let every man go home to his lazy bed.
So we will let this arrogant tyranny continue
until each man is picked off by chance. But if these conditions
(as I am sure they do) have enough fire in them
to kindle even cowards to action, and to make
even the passive spirits of women courageous; then, my
          fellow Romans,
what spur other than our own cause do we need
to incite us to remedy these conditions? What other bond
than that of Romans able to keep a secret, who have
          pledged their word
and will not be deceitful? And what other oath
than the personal honor of man to man
that this will be or we will die in the attempt?
Let priests swear and cowards and deceivers and
feeble old men and such patient souls
who actually welcome wrongs. In evil causes, let
such creatures swear whom everyone is doubtful of, but
          do not stain
the unspotted virtue of our enterprise,
nor the unbeatable courage of our spirits,
by thinking that either our cause or our performance of it
requires an oath—when every drop of blood
that flows in every Roman's veins, and nobly flows,
will show that it is not of Roman origin
if he breaks the smallest particle
of any promise that he has given.

CASSIUS

But what about Cicero? Shall we sound him out?
I think he will be a very strong asset for us.

CASCA

Let us not leave him out.

CINNA

No, by no means.

METELLUS

 O let us have him, for his silver hairs*

145 Will purchase us a good opinion,

 And buy men's voices to commend our deeds.

 It shall be said his judgment ruled our hands.

 Our youths and wildness shall no whit appear,

 But all be buried in his gravity.

BRUTUS

150 O name him not; let us not break with him,

 For he will never follow anything

 That other men begin.

CASSIUS

       Then leave him out.

CASCA

 Indeed, he is not fit.

DECIUS

 Shall no man else be touched, but only Caesar?

CASSIUS

155 Decius, well urged. I think it is not meet

 Mark Antony, so well beloved of Caesar,

 Should outlive Caesar; we shall find of him

 A shrewd contriver. And you know, his means,

 If he improve them, may well stretch so far

160 As to annoy us all; which to prevent,

 Let Antony and Caesar fall together.

BRUTUS

 Our course will seem too bloody, Caius Cassius,

 To cut the head off and then hack the limbs—

 Like wrath in death and envy afterwards;

165 For Antony is but a limb of Caesar.

 Let's be sacrificers, but not butchers, Caius.

 We all stand up against the spirit of Caesar,

 And in the spirit of men there is no blood.

 O that we then could come by Caesar's spirit

 And not dismember Caesar! But, alas,

 Caesar must bleed for it. And, gentle* friends,

 Let's kill him boldly, but not wrathfully;

---

144 *silver hairs* a reference both to Cicero's age and to his reputation for dignity (from the purity and brightness of silver). Metellus is also thinking of silver as a word for money (note "purchase" and "buy" in the next lines), perhaps as the price of betrayal, as Judas betrayed Christ for thirty pieces of silver.

METELLUS

    O let us have him, because his silvery hair

145   will win us everyone's good opinion

    and buy men's speeches to praise our deeds.

    It shall be said that his good judgment guided our hands.

    Our youth and wildness won't show at all,

    but everything will be covered over by Cicero's

        solid respectability.

BRUTUS

    O don't mention Cicero's name. Let us not disclose our

150   plans to him,

    for he will never follow any cause

    started by other men.

CASSIUS

    Then leave him out.

CASCA

    Indeed, he is not suitable.

DECIUS

    Don't we plan to take care of anyone else besides Caesar?

CASSIUS

155   A point well taken, Decius. I don't think it's right

    that Mark Antony, so well loved by Caesar,

    should live after Caesar is dead. We shall find that he is

    a dangerous plotter. And you know his resources,

    if he makes good use of them, may be so extensive

160   as to harm us all. To prevent this,

    let Antony and Caesar be struck down together.

BRUTUS

    Our acts will seem too bloody, Caius Cassius,

    to cut off the head of the state, and then start hacking away

      the limbs—

    as if we put Caesar to death in anger, then showed a malicious

      spirit afterwards,

165   since Antony is only a limb of Caesar.

    Let's be sacrificers, but not butchers, Caius.

    We are all fighting against the spirit of Caesar,

    and in the spirit of men there is no blood.

    O that we then could get hold of Caesar's spirit

170   without cutting him up! But, alas,

    Caesar must bleed. And, noble friends,

    let's kill him boldly, but not in anger;

---

171 *gentle* wordplay on two senses: 1) having the quality of a gentleman, noble; 2) not harsh or violent. It is a typical irony of Brutus that he
hould call his friends "gentle" in the very sentence that he is asking them to
'l Caesar.

Let's carve him as a dish fit for the gods,
Not hew him as a carcass fit for hounds.
175   And let our hearts, as subtle masters do,
Stir up their servants to an act of rage,
And after seem to chide 'em. This shall make
Our purpose necessary, and not envious;
Which so appearing to the common eyes,
180   We shall be called purgers, not murderers.
And for Mark Antony, think not of him;
For he can do no more than Caesar's arm
When Caesar's head is off.

CASSIUS
                              Yet I fear him,
For in the ingrafted love he bears to Caesar—

BRUTUS
185   Alas, good Cassius, do not think of him.
If he love Caesar, all that he can do
Is to himself: take thought and die for Caesar;
And that were much he should, for he is given
To sports, to wildness, and much company.

TREBONIUS
190   There is no fear in him; let him not die,
For he will live, and laugh at this hereafter.
         Clock strikes.

BRUTUS
Peace! Count the clock.

CASSIUS
                              The clock hath stricken three.

TREBONIUS
'Tis time to part.

CASSIUS
                    But it is doubtful yet
Whether Caesar will come forth today or no;
195   For he is superstitious grown of late,
Quite from the main opinion he held once
Of fantasy, of dreams, and ceremonies.

let's carve him up like a dish sacrificed to the gods,
not hack him to pieces as if he were a carcass thrown
    to the hounds.

175 And let our hearts, like cunning masters,
incite their servants to an angry and violent deed
and afterwards pretend to scold them for it. This shall make
what we have to do necessary and not spiteful;
which, by so appearing to the ordinary people,
we shall be called purgers (who cure their patients
180   by bloodletting), and not murderers.
As for Mark Antony, don't think about him,
because he can accomplish no more than Caesar's arm
after Caesar's head has been cut off.

CASSIUS
I still fear him,
because the deeply felt love he bears to Caesar—

BRUTUS
185 Alas, good Cassius, do not think about him.
If he really loves Caesar, he can only express it
personally, by becoming melancholy and letting himself die
    for Caesar's sake.
And that would be far beyond his capacity, because he is
    much addicted
to sports, to wildness, and to the enjoyment of his
    friends' company.

TREBONIUS
190 There is nothing to be feared in Antony. Don't let him die,
and you'll see that he will live to laugh at this matter afterwards.
    Clock strikes.

BRUTUS
Silence! Count the strokes of the clock.

CASSIUS
The clock has struck three.

TREBONIUS
It's time to leave.

CASSIUS
But it is still doubtful
whether Caesar will go out today,
195 because he has recently become superstitious—
very different from the way he used to think about
imaginary fears, dreams, and bad omens.

It may be these apparent prodigies,
The unaccustomed terror of this night,
200 And the persuasion of his augurers,
May hold him from the Capitol today.

DECIUS
Never fear that. If he be so resolved,
I can o'ersway him; for he loves to hear
That unicorns may be betrayed with trees,
205 And bears with glasses, elephants with holes,
Lions with toils, and men with flatterers.
But when I tell him he hates flatterers,
He says he does, being then most flatterèd.
Let me work;
210 For I can give his humor the true bent,
And I will bring him to the Capitol.

CASSIUS
Nay, we will all of us be there to fetch him.

BRUTUS
By the eighth hour; is that the uttermost?

CINNA
Be that the uttermost, and fail not then.

METELLUS
215 Caius Ligarius doth bear Caesar hard,
Who rated him for speaking well of Pompey.
I wonder none of you have thought of him.

BRUTUS
Now, good Metellus, go along by him.
He loves me well, and I have given him reasons;
220 Send him but hither, and I'll fashion him.

CASSIUS
The morning comes upon's. We'll leave you, Brutus.
And, friends, disperse yourselves; but all remember
What you have said, and show yourselves true Romans.

BRUTUS
Good gentlemen, look fresh and merrily.
225 Let not our looks put on our purposes,
But bear it as our Roman actors do,
With untired spirits and formal constancy.

It may be that these undisputed wonders,
the extraordinary terror of this night,
200 and the persuasion of his fortune-tellers
may keep him from the Capitol today.

DECIUS
Don't ever fear that. If he is determined to stay home,
I know how to persuade him to go, because he loves
   to hear stories
about how unicorns may be trapped by impaling their horns
   in trees,
and how bears can be dazzled by mirrors, elephants caught
205   in covered pits,
lions by nets, and men by flatterers.
But when I tell him he hates flatterers,
he says he does, at the very moment he is most flattered.
Let me work on him,
210 because I know how to twist his whims around,
and I guarantee I will bring him to the Capitol.

CASSIUS
No, all of us will be there to get him.

BRUTUS
By eight o'clock. Is that the latest time?

CINNA
Let that be the latest, and don't fail to be there then.

METELLUS
215 Caius Ligarius has a grudge against Caesar,
who rebuked him for speaking well of Pompey—
I wonder why no one has thought about including him.

BRUTUS
Good Metellus, now go to his house.
He loves me well, and I have already given him reasons to join us.
220 Just send him to me, and I'll win him over.

CASSIUS
Morning is near. We'll leave you, Brutus.
And, friends, let's disperse. But all remember
what you have said, and show yourselves true Romans.

BRUTUS
Good gentlemen, look fresh and lively.
Don't let our serious looks reveal our purposes,
225 but let us play it out like Roman actors,
with untired spirits and a dignified self-control.

And so good morrow to you every one.
    Exeunt. BRUTUS *remains.*
Boy! Lucius! Fast asleep? It is no matter;
230   Enjoy the honey-heavy dew of slumber.
Thou hast no figures nor no fantasies
Which busy care draws in the brains of men;
Therefore thou sleep'st so sound.
    Enter PORTIA.

PORTIA
                       Brutus, my lord.

BRUTUS
Portia! What mean you? Wherefore rise you now?
235   It is not for your health thus to commit
Your weak condition to the raw cold morning.

PORTIA
Nor for yours neither. Y'have ungently, Brutus,
Stole from my bed. And yesternight at supper
You suddenly arose and walked about,
240   Musing and sighing, with your arms across;
And when I asked you what the matter was,
You stared upon me with ungentle looks.
I urged you further; then you scratched your head,
And too impatiently stamped with your foot.
245   Yet I insisted, yet you answered not,
But with an angry wafter of your hand
Gave sign for me to leave you. So I did,
Fearing to strengthen that impatience
Which seemed too much enkindled; and withal
250   Hoping it was but an effect of humor,
Which sometime hath his hour with every man.
It will not let you eat, nor talk, nor sleep;
And could it work so much upon your shape
As it hath much prevailed on your condition,
255   I should not know you Brutus. Dear my lord,
Make me acquainted with your cause of grief.

BRUTUS
I am not well in health, and that is all.

And so good morning to every one of you.
> *They exit*; BRUTUS *remains*.

Boy! Lucius! Fast asleep? It doesn't matter;
230   enjoy your deep sleep, heavy like a honeyed dew.
You don't have either the images or the troublesome dreams
that constant worry arouses in the brains of important men—
that's why you can sleep so soundly.
> *Enter* PORTIA.

PORTIA
Portia, my lord.

BRUTUS
Portia! What do you mean by coming here? Why do you
    get up now?
235   It is not good for your health to expose
your delicate constitution to the raw cold morning.

PORTIA
Nor for yours either. You've been discourteous, Brutus,
in stealing away from my bed. And last night at supper
you suddenly got up and walked about,
240   thinking and sighing, with your arms folded across your chest.
And when I asked you what was the matter,
you stared at me with rude looks.
I pressed you further; then you scratched your head,
and stamped your foot impatiently.
245   I still insisted, yet you didn't answer,
but with an angry wave of your hand
you signaled me to leave you. So I did,
afraid to aggravate your bad temper,
which already seemed too much inflamed, and
250   hoping that it was, indeed, just a passing mood
that sometimes affects everyone.
Whatever bothers you will not let you eat, nor talk, nor sleep,
and if it had as strong an effect on your physical appearance
as it seems to dominate your psychological state,
255   I wouldn't be able to recognize you, Brutus. My dear lord,
let me know what's causing your grief.

BRUTUS
I don't feel well, and that is all there is to it.

PORTIA

Brutus is wise and, were he not in health,
He would embrace the means to come by it.

BRUTUS

260   Why, so I do. Good Portia, go to bed.

PORTIA

Is Brutus sick? And is it physical
To walk unbracèd and suck up the humors
Of the dank morning? What, is Brutus sick?
And will he steal out of his wholesome bed
265   To dare the vile contagion of the night,*
And tempt the rheumy and unpurgèd air
To add unto his sickness? No, my Brutus,
You have some sick offense within your mind,
Which by the right and virtue of my place
270   I ought to know of; and upon my knees,
I charm you, by my once commended beauty,
By all your vows of love, and that great vow
Which did incorporate and make us one,
That you unfold to me, your self, your half,
275   Why you are heavy—and what men tonight
Have had resort to you; for here have been
Some six or seven, who did hide their faces
Even from darkness.

BRUTUS

Kneel not, gentle Portia.

PORTIA

I should not need, if you were gentle Brutus.
280   Within the bond of marriage, tell me, Brutus,
Is it excepted I should know no secrets
That appertain to you? Am I your self
But, as it were, in sort or limitation?
To keep with you at meals, comfort your bed,
285   And talk to you sometimes? Dwell I but in the suburbs*
Of your good pleasure? If it be no more,
Portia is Brutus' harlot, not his wife.

---

265 *vile contagion of the night* capacity of the night air to infect. In
Shakespeare's time it was generally believed that the night air could cause
disease.

PORTIA

> Brutus is a wise man, and if he weren't in good health,
> he would take steps to recover.

BRUTUS

260 Why, that's what I'm doing. Good Portia, go to bed.

PORTIA

> Is Brutus sick? And is it good for your health
> to walk with your jacket unbuttoned and inhale the mists
> of the dank morning? What, is Brutus sick?
> And will he steal out of his healthy bed
265 to risk the loathsome contagiousness of the night,
> and tempt the damp and unpurified air that he breathes
> to make his sickness worse? No, my Brutus,
> you have some harmful sickness in your mind,
> which by the rights and obligations of being your wife
270 I ought to know of. And upon my knees
> I beg of you, by my beauty that you once found so praiseworthy,
> by all your vows of love, and that great marriage vow
> which brought us together and united us,
> that you reveal to me—your self, your other half—
275 why you are so depressed. And tell me what men
> have visited you tonight, because there were
> six or seven persons here, who hid their faces
> even from the darkness of the night.

BRUTUS

> Don't kneel, gentle Portia.

PORTIA

> I wouldn't need to if you were gentle Brutus.
280 According to the marriage contract, tell me Brutus,
> is there an exception made that I should know no secrets
> that relate to you? Have I, as your wife, united my self with you
> not absolutely, but only with certain conditions and restrictions?
> To keep you company at meals, to please you in bed,
> and talk to you sometimes? Do I only live in the suburbs
285   and not at the center
> of your wishes and desires? If it's no more than that,
> Portia is Brutus's whore, not his wife.

---

285 *suburbs* the connotation is that of a red-light district, and "suburbs"
leads directly to "harlot" in line 287. The suburbs of London, especially those
of Southwark (the theater district across the Thames River), were notorious
for houses of prostitution.

BRUTUS

You are my true and honorable wife,
As dear to me as are the ruddy drops
290   That visit my sad heart.

PORTIA

If this were true, then should I know this secret.
I grant I am a woman; but withal
A woman that Lord Brutus took to wife.
I grant I am a woman; but withal
295   A woman well reputed, Cato's* daughter.
Think you I am no stronger than my sex,
Being so fathered and so husbanded?
Tell me your counsels, I will not disclose 'em.
I have made strong proof of my constancy,
300   Giving myself a voluntary wound
Here, in the thigh. Can I bear that with patience,
And not my husband's secrets?

BRUTUS

O ye gods!

Render me worthy of this noble wife.
Knock.
Hark, hark, one knocks. Portia, go in awhile,
305   And by and by thy bosom shall partake
The secrets of my heart.
All my engagements I will construe to thee,
All the charactery of my sad brows.
Leave me with haste.
Exit PORTIA.

Lucius, who's that knocks?
Enter LUCIUS *and* LIGARIUS.

LUCIUS

310   Here is a sick man that would speak with you.

BRUTUS

Caius Ligarius, that Metellus spake of.
Boy, stand aside. Caius Ligarius, how?

LIGARIUS

Vouchsafe good morrow from a feeble tongue.

---

295 *Cato's* Marcus Porcius Cato was known, like his great-grandfathe
Cato the Censor, for the strict moral integrity of his life. He was the unc
of Brutus as well as his father-in-law.

BRUTUS
You are my true and honorable wife,
as dear to me as are the red drops of blood
290   that flow through my heavy heart.

PORTIA
If this is true, then I should know your secret.
I admit I am a woman, but also
a woman whom Lord Brutus took for his wife.
I admit I am a woman, but also
295   a woman well thought of, Cato's daughter.
Don't you believe I ought to be stronger than most women,
with such a father and such a husband?
Tell me your secrets; I will not disclose them.
I have proved my strength of character
300   by slashing myself, of my own free will,
here in the thigh. Can I bear that wound without complaining
and not be able to keep my husband's secrets?

BRUTUS
O you gods!
Make me worthy of this noble wife.
        Knock.
Listen, listen, someone knocks. Portia, go inside for a while,
305   and very soon you shall know
the secrets of my heart.
I will explain in detail to you all my commitments,
and all the meaning inscribed in my care-worn face.
Go quickly.
        Exit PORTIA.
Lucius, who's knocking?
        Enter LUCIUS *and* LIGARIUS.

LUCIUS
310   Here is a sick man who wants to speak with you.

BRUTUS
It's Caius Ligarius, whom Metellus spoke of.
Boy, stand aside. Caius Ligarius, how are you?

LIGARIUS
Accept a "good morning" from a feeble tongue.

BRUTUS
O what a time have you chose out, brave Caius,
315   To wear a kerchief! Would you were not sick!

LIGARIUS
I am not sick, if Brutus have in hand
Any exploit worthy the name of honor.

BRUTUS
Such an exploit have I in hand, Ligarius,
Had you a healthful ear to hear of it.

LIGARIUS
320   By all the gods that Romans bow before,
I here discard my sickness. Soul of Rome,
Brave son, derived from honorable loins,
Thou like an exorcist hast conjured up
My mortifièd spirit. Now bid me run,
325   And I will strive with things impossible,
Yea, get the better of them. What's to do?

BRUTUS
A piece of work that will make sick men whole.

LIGARIUS
But are not some whole that we must make sick?

BRUTUS
That must we also. What it is, my Caius,
330   I shall unfold to thee, as we are going
To whom it must be done.

LIGARIUS
                              Set on your foot,
And with a heart new-fired I follow you,
To do I know not what; but it sufficeth
That Brutus leads me on.
          Thunder.

BRUTUS
                              Follow me then.
          Exeunt.

BRUTUS

O what a time you have chosen, brave Caius,
to wrap your head in a bandage! I wish you were not sick!

LIGARIUS

I am not sick any longer if Brutus has
some action worthy the name of honor.

BRUTUS

Such an action is what I am now undertaking, Ligarius,
if you could hear about it with a healthy ear.

LIGARIUS

By all the gods that Romans worship,
I hereby discard my sickness. (*He throws off his bandage and
   addresses Brutus solemnly.*) Soul of Rome,
brave son, descended from honorable ancestors,
like an exorcist you have conjured up
my deadened spirit (and given it new life). Now ask me to run,
and I will fight against impossible things—
yes, and get the better of them, too. What do I have to do?

BRUTUS

A piece of work that will make sick men healthy again.

LIGARIUS

But aren't there some healthy men whom we must make sick?

BRUTUS

That's part of it. What it is we need to do, my Caius,
I shall reveal to you while we are going
to the person to whom it must be done.

LIGARIUS

Lead the way,
and with a spirit that has just been inspired by your words,
   I will follow you,
to do I don't know what, but it's enough for me
that Brutus leads me on.
      Thunder.

BRUTUS

Follow me then.
      They exit.

[Scene ii: Rome, Caesar's house.] *Thunder and lightning. Enter*
JULIUS CAESAR *in his nightgown.*

CAESAR

Nor heaven nor earth have been at peace tonight.
Thrice hath Calphurnia in her sleep cried out,
"Help, ho! They murder Caesar!" Who's within?
     Enter a Servant.

SERVANT

My lord.

CAESAR

5   Go bid the priests do present sacrifice,*
And bring me their opinions of success.

SERVANT

I will, my lord.
          Exit.
          Enter CALPHURNIA.

CALPHURNIA

What mean you, Caesar? Think you to walk forth?
You shall not stir out of your house today.

CAESAR

10   Caesar shall forth; the things that threatened me
Ne'er looked but on my back. When they shall see
The face of Caesar, they are vanishèd.

CALPHURNIA

Caesar, I never stood on ceremonies,
Yet now they fright me. There is one within,
15   Besides the things that we have heard and seen,
Recounts most horrid sights seen by the watch.
A lioness hath whelpèd in the streets,
And graves have yawned and yielded up their dead.
Fierce fiery warriors fight upon the clouds
20   In ranks and squadrons and right form of war,
Which drizzled blood upon the Capitol.
The noise of battle hurtled in the air,
Horses did neigh, and dying men did groan,
And ghosts did shriek and squeal about the streets.
25   O Caesar, these things are beyond all use,
And I do fear them.

---

5 *sacrifice* Roman priests sacrificed various animals and examined their
inner organs as a way of predicting the future. Many other forms of fore-
casting were practiced, such as studying the flight of birds.

Scene ii: Rome, Caesar's house. Thunder and lightning continue.
Enter JULIUS CAESAR *in his dressing gown.*

CAESAR
Neither heaven nor earth has been quiet tonight.
Calphurnia cried out three times in her sleep,
"Help, there! They are murdering Caesar!" Who's on
    duty inside?
      Enter a Servant.

SERVANT
My lord.

CAESAR
5   Go tell the priests to sacrifice an animal right away,
and bring me their opinion about the outcome.

SERVANT
I will, my lord.
    Exit.
    Enter CALPHURNIA.

CALPHURNIA
What do you mean to do, Caesar? Are you thinking of going out?
I won't allow you to stir out of the house today.

CAESAR
10   Caesar will go out. The things that threatened me
came at me from behind. When they shall see
the face of Caesar, they will be forced to vanish.

CALPHURNIA
Caesar, I never gave much importance to signs and omens,
yet now they frighten me. There is someone in the house who,
15   besides the things that we have heard and seen,
tells about horrible sights seen by the watchmen.
A lioness has littered right in the streets,
and graves have opened and given up their dead.
Fierce fiery warriors fought in the clouds
20   in ranks and squadrons and proper military order,
and their conflict drizzled blood onto the Capitol.
The noise of battle clashed in the air,
horses neighed, dying men groaned,
and ghosts shrieked and squealed as they went about the streets.
O Caesar, these things are strange and abnormal,
and I fear them.

CAESAR
>   What can be avoided
> Whose end is purposed by the mighty gods?
> Yet Caesar shall go forth; for these predictions
> Are to the world in general as to Caesar.

CALPHURNIA
> When beggars die, there are no comets seen;
> The heavens themselves blaze forth the death of princes.

CAESAR
> Cowards die many times before their deaths;
> The valiant never taste of death but once.
> Of all the wonders that I yet have heard,
> It seems to me most strange that men should fear,
> Seeing that death, a necessary end,
> Will come when it will come.

> *Enter a Servant.*

>   What say the augurers?

SERVANT
> They would not have you to stir forth today.
> Plucking the entrails of an offering forth,
> They could not find a heart within the beast.

CAESAR
> The gods do this in shame of cowardice.
> Caesar should be a beast without a heart
> If he should stay at home today for fear.
> No, Caesar shall not. Danger knows full well
> That Caesar is more dangerous than he.
> We are two lions littered in one day,
> And I the elder and more terrible,
> And Caesar shall go forth.

CALPHURNIA
>   Alas, my lord,
> Your wisdom is consumed in confidence.
> Do not go forth today. Call it my fear
> That keeps you in the house, and not your own.
> We'll send Mark Antony to the Senate House,
> And he shall say you are not well today.
> Let me upon my knee prevail in this.

CAESAR
How can anything
the mighty gods intend to inflict on us be avoided?
Even so, Caesar will go out, because these predictions
apply to everyone in general as well as to Caesar.

CALPHURNIA
30   When beggars die, there is no grand display of comets,
but for the death of princes the heavens make a blazing show.

CAESAR
Cowards die many times before their deaths;
valiant men only taste death once.
Of all the amazing things I've heard about,
35   it seems to me very strange that men should be afraid,
seeing that death, the necessary end of all,
will come when it will come.
          Enter a Servant.
What do the fortune-tellers have to say?

SERVANT
They don't want you to venture out of your house today.
While plucking out the guts of an offering,
40   they could not find a heart within the beast.

CAESAR
The gods do this to put cowards to shame.
Caesar, too, would be a beast without a heart
if he should stay at home today from fear.
No, Caesar won't do that. Danger itself knows very well
45   that Caesar is more dangerous than he.
We are two lions born on the same day,
and I am the elder and more terrible—
and Caesar *will* go out.

CALPHURNIA
Alas, my lord,
your wisdom is devoured by over-confidence.
50   Do not go out today. Say it's my fear
that keeps you in the house and not your own.
We'll send Mark Antony to the Senate House,
and he shall say you are not well today.
I go down on my knees to win you over in this.

CAESAR
55   Mark Antony shall say I am not well,
       And for thy humor I will stay at home.
               Enter DECIUS.
       Here's Decius Brutus, he shall tell them so.

DECIUS
       Caesar, all hail! Good morrow, worthy Caesar;
       I come to fetch you to the Senate House.

CAESAR
60   And you are come in very happy time
       To bear my greeting to the senators
       And tell them that I will not come today.
       Cannot, is false; and that I dare not, falser.
       I will not come today; tell them so, Decius.

CALPHURNIA
       Say he is sick.

CAESAR
65   Shall Caesar send a lie?
       Have I in conquest stretched mine arm so far
       To be afeard to tell graybeards the truth?
       Decius, go tell them Caesar will not come.

DECIUS
       Most mighty Caesar, let me know some cause,
70   Lest I be laughed at when I tell them so.

CAESAR
       The cause is in my will: I will not come;
       That is enough to satisfy the Senate.
       But for your private satisfaction,
       Because I love you, I will let you know.
75   Calphurnia here, my wife, stays me at home.
       She dreamt tonight she saw my statue,
       Which, like a fountain, with an hundred spouts
       Did run pure blood; and many lusty Romans
       Came smiling and did bathe their hands in it.
80   And these does she apply for warnings and portents
       And evils imminent; and on her knee
       Hath begged that I will stay at home today.

CAESAR

55   All right, Mark Antony shall say I am not well,
    and because of your whim I will stay at home.
         Enter DECIUS.
    Here's Decius Brutus. He shall tell them so.

DECIUS

    Caesar, I salute you! Good morning, worthy Caesar;
    I come to accompany you to the Senate House.

CAESAR

60   And you have come just at the right moment
    to take my greeting to the senators
    and tell them that I will not come today.
    I won't say "cannot"—that's false, and that I dare not go
        is even falser.
    I will not come today; tell them so, Decius.

CALPHURNIA

    Say he is sick.

CAESAR

65   Shall Caesar send a lie?
    Have I in conquest done such mighty deeds
    that I am afraid to tell old men the truth?
    Decius, go tell them Caesar will not come.

DECIUS

    Most mighty Caesar, give me some reason,
70   so they won't laugh at me when I tell them.

CAESAR

    My will is the reason: I will not come;
    that is enough to satisfy the Senate.
    But for your private information,
    because I love you, I will tell you the truth.
75   Calphurnia here, my wife, keeps me at home.
    She dreamt last night that she saw my statue,
    which—like a fountain with a hundred spouts—
    spurted pure blood. And many high-spirited Romans
    came smiling and bathed their hands in it.
80   And these signs she interprets as warnings and bad omens
    of evil things about to occur; and on her knees
    has begged that I will stay at home today.

DECIUS
    This dream is all amiss interpreted;
    It was a vision fair and fortunate.
85   Your statue spouting blood in many pipes,
    In which so many smiling Romans bathed,
    Signifies that from you great Rome shall suck
    Reviving blood, and that great men shall press
    For tinctures, stains, relics, and cognizance.*
90   This by Calphurnia's dream is signified.

CAESAR
    And this way have you well expounded it.

DECIUS
    I have, when you have heard what I can say—
    And know it now: the Senate have concluded
    To give this day a crown to mighty Caesar.
95   If you shall send them word you will not come,
    Their minds may change. Besides, it were a mock
    Apt to be rendered, for some one to say,
    "Break up the Senate till another time,
    When Caesar's wife shall meet with better dreams."
100   If Caesar hide himself, shall they not whisper,
    "Lo, Caesar is afraid"?
    Pardon me, Caesar, for my dear dear love
    To your proceeding bids me tell you this;
    And reason to my love is liable.

CAESAR
105   How foolish do your fears seem now, Calphurnia!
    I am ashamèd I did yield to them.
    Give me my robe, for I will go.
           Enter BRUTUS, LIGARIUS, METELLUS, CASCA,
           TREBONIUS, CINNA, *and* PUBLIUS.
    And look where Publius is come to fetch me.

PUBLIUS
    Good morrow, Caesar.

CAESAR
                Welcome, Publius.
110   What, Brutus, are you stirred so early too?

---

   89 *tinctures . . . cognizance* In alchemy, "tinctures" are quintessences
or elixirs, and in heraldry, the materials used in preparing a coat of arms.
"Stains" are heraldic colors; very close in meaning to "tinctures." "Cog-

DECIUS

   This interpretation of the dream is completely wrong—
   it was a beautiful vision, promising good fortune.
85   Your statue spouting blood from many pipes,
   in which so many smiling Romans bathed their hands,
   is a sign that great Rome will get from you the blood
   that will revive her, and that great men shall be eager to have
   handkerchiefs dipped in your blood, as holy souvenirs to venerate,
      and bloody badges to show that they are your followers.
90   This is the true meaning of Calphurnia's dream.

CAESAR

   Your explanation is convincing.

DECIUS

   I agree, especially when you have heard what I am about to say—
   and know the good news now: the Senate has decided
   to give a crown today to mighty Caesar.
95   If you shall send them word you will not come,
   they may change their minds. Besides, it would be an easy insult
   for some one to say,
   "Adjourn the Senate to another time,
   when Caesar's wife has better dreams."
100   If Caesar hides himself, won't the senators whisper,
   "Lo, Caesar is afraid"?
   Pardon me, Caesar, for it is only my dearest love
   of your career that makes me tell you this;
   I wouldn't give you my reasons so frankly if I didn't love you.

CAESAR

105   How foolish your fears seem now, Calphurnia!
   I am ashamed of myself for giving way to them.
   Give me my toga, because I will go to the Senate.
      Enter BRUTUS, LIGARIUS, METELLUS, CASCA,
      TREBONIUS, CINNA, *and* PUBLIUS.
   And look where Publius has come to accompany me.

PUBLIUS

   Good morning, Caesar.

CAESAR

   Welcome, Publius.
110   What, Brutus, are you up so early too?

---

nizance" means "an heraldic device or emblem worn by a nobleman's followers."

Good morrow, Casca. Caius Ligarius,
Caesar was ne'er so much your enemy*
As that same ague which hath made you lean.
What is't a clock?

BRUTUS
                              Caesar, 'tis strucken eight.

CAESAR
115   I thank you for your pains and courtesy.

        Enter ANTONY.

See, Antony, that revels long a-nights,
Is notwithstanding up. Good morrow, Antony.

ANTONY
So to most noble Caesar.

CAESAR
                              Bid them prepare within.
I am to blame to be thus waited for.
120   Now Cinna, now Metellus. What, Trebonius,
I have an hour's talk in store for you;
Remember that you call on me today;
Be near me, that I may remember you.

TREBONIUS
Caesar, I will. [*Aside*] And so near will I be,
125   That your best friends shall wish I had been further.

CAESAR
Good friends, go in and taste some wine with me,
And we, like friends, will straightway go together.

BRUTUS
[*Aside*] That every like is not the same,* O Caesar,
The heart of Brutus earns to think upon.
        Exeunt.

[*Scene iii: Rome, a street.*] *Enter* ARTEMIDORUS, [*reading a paper*].

ARTEMIDORUS
"Caesar, beware of Brutus; take heed of Cassius; come not near
Casca; have an eye to Cinna; trust not Trebonius; mark well
Metellus Cimber; Decius Brutus loves thee not; thou hast wronged

---

112 *enemy* Ligarius had supported Pompey against Caesar in the Civil
War and had recently been pardoned by Caesar and restored to civil rights.
128 *That . . . same* Brutus picks up Caesar's phrase, "like friends," and
plays on the distinction between "like" and "same," similarity and identity.

Good morning, Casca. Caius Ligarius,
Caesar was never your enemy so much
as that fever which has made you lean.
What time is it?

BRUTUS

Caesar, it has struck eight.

CAESAR *(to all)*

115   I thank you for the pains you have taken and your courtesy.
Enter ANTONY.
See, even Antony, who stays out late partying,
is also up. Good morning, Antony.

ANTONY

Good morning to most noble Caesar.

CAESAR

Ask the servants to prepare some wine.
I am ashamed to keep you waiting for me.

120   Good morning, Cinna and Metellus. Just a moment, Trebonius,
I have an hour's chat ready for you.
Remember to speak to me today;
stay near me, so that I can remind myself to do you some favor.

TREBONIUS

Caesar, I will. *(To the audience, ironically)* And I will be
so near you

125   that your best friends will wish I had been further away.

CAESAR

Good friends, come in and taste some wine with me,
and we, like friends, will soon go to the Senate together.

BRUTUS *(to the audience)*

That every "like" doesn't mean the same, O Caesar,
the heart of Brutus grieves to think upon.
They exit.

Scene iii: A street in Rome. Enter ARTEMIDORUS, *reading from
a sheet of paper.*

ARTEMIDORUS

"Caesar, beware of Brutus; pay attention to Cassius;
don't go near
Casca; keep an eye on Cinna; don't trust Trebonius; watch
Metellus Cimber carefully; Decius Brutus doesn't love you;
you have wronged

---

appearance and reality. The aside is ironic, since Brutus's understanding of
"like" is not the "same" as Caesar's. In other words, all uses of the word
"like" do not have the "same" meaning.

Caius Ligarius. There is but one mind in all these men, and it is
bent against Caesar. If thou beest not immortal, look about you.
Security gives way to conspiracy. The mighty gods defend thee!
    Thy lover, ARTEMIDORUS."
Here will I stand till Caesar pass along,
And as a suitor will I give him this.
My heart laments that virtue cannot live
Out of the teeth of emulation.
If thou read this, O Caesar, thou mayest live;
If not, the Fates* with traitors do contrive.
    Exit.

[*Scene iv: Rome, before the house of Brutus.*] *Enter* PORTIA *and*
LUCIUS.

PORTIA
  I prithee, boy, run to the Senate House;
  Stay not to answer me, but get thee gone.
  Why dost thou stay?
LUCIUS
              To know my errand, madam.
PORTIA
  I would have had thee there and here again
  Ere I can tell thee what thou shouldst do there.
  [*Aside*] O Constancy, be strong upon my side,
  Set a huge mountain 'tween my heart and tongue.
  I have a man's mind, but a woman's might.
  How hard it is for women to keep counsel!*
  —Art thou here yet?
LUCIUS
            Madam, what should I do?
  Run to the Capitol, and nothing else?
  And so return to you, and nothing else?
PORTIA
  Yes, bring me word, boy, if thy lord look well,
  For he went sickly forth; and take good note
  What Caesar doth, what suitors press to him.
  Hark, boy, what noise is that?

---

13 *Fates* in Greek mythology, the three goddesses who ruled the lives
and destinies of men: Clotho, who spun the web of life; Lachesis, who measured out its length; and Atropos, who cut it off at death.
II,iv
9 *How . . . counsel* It is apparent that Brutus has revealed his secrets to
Portia, as he promised to do at the end of Act II, Scene i. But Portia'

Caius Ligarius. All these men think the same way about you,
    and they are all
dead-set against Caesar. If you're not immortal, look about
5   you diligently.
Overconfidence opens the way for conspiracy. May the mighty
    gods protect you!
            Your devoted friend, ARTEMIDORUS."
I will stand here until Caesar passes by,
and as a petitioner I will give him this paper.
10 My heart grieves that goodness cannot live
out of the reach of jealousy's envious fangs.
If you read this message, O Caesar, you may live;
if not, the Fates conspire with traitors to destroy you.
        Exit.

Scene iv: Rome, before the house of BRUTUS. *Enter* PORTIA
and LUCIUS.

PORTIA
    Please, boy, run to the Senate House.
    Don't stay to answer me, but get going.
    Why do you remain here?
LUCIUS
    To know what my errand is, madam.
PORTIA
    I would have liked you to be there and back again
5   before I told you what you should do there.
    (*To herself*) O may I be able to maintain my self-control!
    Set a huge mountain between my heart and tongue!
    I have the mind of a man, but the strength of a woman.
    How hard it is for women to keep a secret.
    (*To Lucius*) Are you still here?
LUCIUS
10 Madam, what should I do?
    Just run to the Capitol, and nothing else?
    And then return to you, and nothing else?
PORTIA
    Yes, bring me word, boy, if your lord Brutus looks well,
    because he was sick when he left. And observe carefully
    what Caesar does, what suitors crowd around him.
    Listen, boy, what noise is that?

---

manly resolution, as demonstrated by the "voluntary wound" she has given
herself "Here, in the thigh" (2.1.300-1), seems to be breaking down in Act II,
Scene iv, where she is much troubled by the conflict of conventional male and
female roles. The pressure of events is finally too much for Portia, who becomes deranged and commits suicide by swallowing live coals (as reported in
4.3.150-54).

LUCIUS
    I hear none, madam.
PORTIA
                                    Prithee listen well.
    I heard a bustling rumor like a fray,
    And the wind brings it from the Capitol.
LUCIUS
20   Sooth, madam, I hear nothing.
            Enter the Soothsayer.
PORTIA
    Come hither, fellow. Which way hast thou been?
SOOTHSAYER
    At mine own house, good lady.
PORTIA
    What is't a clock?
SOOTHSAYER
                            About the ninth hour, lady.
PORTIA
    Is Caesar yet gone to the Capitol?
SOOTHSAYER
25   Madam, not yet. I go to take my stand,
    To see him pass on to the Capitol.
PORTIA
    Thou hast some suit to Caesar, hast thou not?
SOOTHSAYER
    That I have, lady, if it will please Caesar
    To be so good to Caesar as to hear me.
30   I shall beseech him to befriend himself.
PORTIA
    Why, know'st thou any harm's intended towards him?
SOOTHSAYER
    None that I know will be, much that I fear may chance.
    Good morrow to you. Here the street is narrow.
    The throng that follows Caesar at the heels,
35   Of senators, of praetors, common suitors,
    Will crowd a feeble man almost to death.
    I'll get me to a place more void, and there
    Speak to great Caesar as he comes along.
            Exit.

LUCIUS
> I hear none, madam.

PORTIA
> Please listen attentively.
> I heard a confused and agitated noise like a street brawl,
> and the wind brings it from the Capitol.

LUCIUS
20
> Truly, madam, I hear nothing.
>> *Enter the Fortune-Teller.*

PORTIA
> Come here, fellow. From what direction are you coming?

FORTUNE-TELLER
> From my own house, good lady.

PORTIA
> What time is it?

FORTUNE-TELLER
> About nine o'clock.

PORTIA
> Has Caesar gone to the Capitol yet?

FORTUNE-TELLER
25
> Madam, not yet. I am going to take up my position
> to see him walk by on the way to the Capitol.

PORTIA
> You have some request of Caesar, don't you?

FORTUNE-TELLER
> I have, lady, if it will please Caesar
> to be so good to himself as to listen to me.
30
> I shall beg him to be a friend to himself.

PORTIA
> Why, are you aware of any harm that's intended for him?

FORTUNE-TELLER
> None that I know will definitely occur, but much that I fear
>> may happen.
> Good morning to you. Here the street is narrow.
> The mob that follows at Caesar's heels,
35
> of senators, of magistrates, and other common suitors,
> will almost crowd a feeble man like myself to death.
> I'll move to a more open place, and there
> speak to great Caesar as he comes by.
>> *Exit.*

PORTIA

[*Aside*] I must go in. Ay me, how weak a thing

40 The heart of woman is! O Brutus,

The heavens speed thee in thine enterprise.

Sure the boy heard me. Brutus hath a suit

That Caesar will not grant. O I grow faint.

—Run, Lucius, and commend me to my lord;

45 Say I am merry. Come to me again,

And bring me word what he doth say to thee.

   Exeunt [*at different doors*].

Act III, [*Scene i: Rome, before the Capitol*]. *Flourish. Enter*
CAESAR, BRUTUS, CASSIUS, CASCA, DECIUS, METELLUS, TREBONIUS,
CINNA, ANTONY, LEPIDUS, ARTEMIDORUS, PUBLIUS, [POPILIUS,] *and
the Soothsayer.*

CAESAR

The ides of March are come.

SOOTHSAYER

Ay, Caesar, but not gone.

ARTEMIDORUS

Hail, Caesar! Read this schedule.

DECIUS

Trebonius doth desire you to o'erread,

5 At your best leisure, this his humble suit.

ARTEMIDORUS

O Caesar, read mine first; for mine's a suit

That touches Caesar nearer. Read it, great Caesar.

CAESAR

What touches us ourself shall be last served.

ARTEMIDORUS

Delay not, Caesar, read it instantly.

CAESAR

What, is the fellow mad?

PUBLIUS

10   Sirrah, give place.

PORTIA

40   (*To herself*) I must go in to the house. O me, how weak a thing
the heart of a woman is! O Brutus,
may the heavens make you successful in your action.
Surely the boy heard me. Brutus wants something from Caesar
that Caesar cannot possibly grant. O I'm feeling faint.
45   (*To Lucius*) Run, Lucius, and send my regards to my lord Brutus.
Say I am joyful. Come back to me again,
and let me know what Brutus says to you.

       PORTIA *and* LUCIUS *exit at opposite sides of the stage.*

*Act III, Scene i: In front of the Capitol building in Rome. A
trumpet fanfare. Enter* CAESAR, BRUTUS, CASSIUS, CASCA,
DECIUS, METELLUS, TREBONIUS, CINNA, ANTONY, LEPI-
DUS, ARTEMIDORUS, PUBLIUS, POPILIUS, *and the Fortune-
Teller.*

CAESAR

    The ides of March have come.

FORTUNE-TELLER

    Yes, Caesar, but they haven't gone.

ARTEMIDORUS

    Hail, Caesar! Read this note.

DECIUS

5   Trebonius wishes you to read,
when you have a chance, this humble request of his.

ARTEMIDORUS

    O Caesar, read mine first, because mine's a matter
that concerns Caesar personally. Read it, great Caesar.

CAESAR

    What concerns me personally shall be considered last.

ARTEMIDORUS

    Don't delay, Caesar, read it instantly.

CAESAR

    What, is the man mad?

PUBLIUS

10   Fellow, get out of the way.

CASSIUS
> What, urge you your petitions in the street?
> Come to the Capitol.
>> [CAESAR *enters the Capitol, the rest following.*]

POPILIUS
> I wish your enterprise today may thrive.

CASSIUS
> What enterprise, Popilius?

POPILIUS
>   Fare you well.
>> [*Advances to* CAESAR.]

BRUTUS
15
> What said Popilius Lena?

CASSIUS
> He wished today our enterprise might thrive.
> I fear our purpose is discoverèd.

BRUTUS
> Look how he makes to Caesar. Mark him.

CASSIUS
> Casca, be sudden, for we fear prevention.
20
> Brutus, what shall be done? If this be known,
> Cassius or Caesar never shall turn back,
> For I will slay myself.

BRUTUS
>   Cassius, be constant.
> Popilius Lena speaks not of our purposes;
> For look, he smiles, and Caesar doth not change.

CASSIUS
25
> Trebonius knows his time; for look you, Brutus,
> He draws Mark Antony out of the way.
>> [*Exeunt* ANTONY *and* TREBONIUS.]

DECIUS
> Where is Metellus Cimber? Let him go
> And presently prefer his suit to Caesar.

BRUTUS
> He is addressed. Press near and second him.

CINNA
30
> Casca, you are the first that rears your hand.

CASSIUS

What, are you asking for favors right in the street?
Come in to the Capitol.

> CAESAR *enters the Capitol with his followers.*

POPILIUS

I wish your business today may have good success.

CASSIUS

What "business," Popilius?

POPILIUS

Farewell.

> *Walks up to* CAESAR.

BRUTUS

15 What did Popilius Lena say?

CASSIUS

He wished that our business today might succeed.
I'm afraid that our purpose has been revealed.

BRUTUS

Look how he approaches Caesar. Watch him carefully.

CASSIUS

Casca, be quick, because we fear that we have been found out.
20 Brutus, what shall be done? If our plot is known,
either Cassius or Caesar will never return home alive,
because I will kill myself.

BRUTUS

Cassius, be strong-hearted.
Popilius Lena doesn't speak about our purposes,
because look, he smiles, and Caesar's expression remains
    the same.

CASSIUS

25 Trebonius knows the right moment; see, Brutus,
he draws Mark Antony away from Caesar.

> ANTONY *and* TREBONIUS *exit.*

DECIUS

Where is Metellus Cimber? Let him go
and present his request to Caesar right away.

BRUTUS

He is ready. Go near him and support him.

CINNA

30 Casca, you shall strike the first blow.

CAESAR

> Are we all ready? What is now amiss
> That Caesar and his Senate must redress?

METELLUS

> Most high, most mighty, and most puissant Caesar,
> Metellus Cimber throws before thy seat
> An humble heart.

CAESAR

35   I must prevent thee, Cimber.
> These couchings and these lowly courtesies
> Might fire the blood of ordinary men
> And turn preordinance and first decree
> Into the law of children.* Be not fond
40 To think that Caesar bears such rebel blood
> That will be thawed from the true quality
> With that which melteth fools; I mean sweet words,
> Low-crookèd curtsies, and base spaniel fawning.
> Thy brother by decree is banishèd.
45 If thou dost bend and pray and fawn for him,
> I spurn thee like a cur out of my way.
> Know, Caesar doth not wrong, nor without cause
> Will he be satisfied.

METELLUS

> Is there no voice more worthy than my own
50 To sound more sweetly in great Caesar's ear
> For the repealing of my banished brother?

BRUTUS

> I kiss thy hand, but not in flattery, Caesar;
> Desiring thee that Publius Cimber may
> Have an immediate freedom of repeal.

CAESAR

> What, Brutus?

CASSIUS

55   Pardon, Caesar; Caesar, pardon.
> As low as to thy foot doth Cassius fall
> To beg enfranchisement for Publius Cimber.

---

39 *law of children* The phrase has religious overtones: i.e., the divinely
ordained order of the universe is being converted into the merely capricious

CAESAR
>Are we all ready? What wrong is there now
>that Caesar and his Senate must correct?

METELLUS
>Most high, most mighty, and most powerful Caesar,
>Metellus Cimber kneels humbly
>before you.

CAESAR
35
>I have to cut you off, Cimber.
>These bowings and these servile courtesies
>might stir the passions of ordinary men,
>and turn the natural laws of the universe and the first decree
>   of the gods
>into a merely childish set of rules. Don't be so foolish
>as to think that Caesar has such a wild and highly
40
>   emotional nature
>that will be swayed from its true purpose
>by appeals that move fools—I mean flattery,
>exaggerated bows, and the base, slobbery fawning of a spaniel.
>Your brother is banished by legal decree.
45
>If you choose to bend and pray and fawn for him,
>I will kick you out of my path like a detestable dog.
>Know this: Caesar doesn't commit any wrongs, nor will
>   he seek satisfaction by law
>without reasonable cause.

METELLUS
>Is there any worthier voice than mine
50
>to plead more eloquently in great Caesar's ear
>to recall my brother from exile?

BRUTUS
>I kiss your hand, but not to flatter you, Caesar,
>desiring that Publius Cimber may
>immediately be recalled from exile.

CAESAR
>What, Brutus?

CASSIUS
>Pardon, Caesar; Caesar, pardon.
>Cassius bows down as low as your foot
>to beg a reprieve for Publius Cimber.

---

impulses that motivate children. "Law" is Samuel Johnson's emendation for
"lane" in the Folio.

CAESAR

I could be well moved, if I were as you;
If I could pray to move, prayers would move me.
60   But I am constant as the Northern Star,
Of whose true-fixed and resting quality
There is no fellow in the firmament.
The skies are painted with unnumb'red sparks,
They are all fire, and every one doth shine;
65   But there's but one in all doth hold his place.
So in the world: 'tis furnished well with men,
And men are flesh and blood, and apprehensive;
Yet in the number I do know but one
That unassailable holds on his rank,
70   Unshaked of motion; and that I am he,
Let me a little show it, even in this:
That I was constant Cimber should be banished,
And constant do remain to keep him so.

CINNA

O Caesar—

CAESAR

Hence! Wilt thou lift up Olympus?*

DECIUS

Great Caesar—

CAESAR

75   Doth not Brutus bootless kneel?

CASCA

Speak hands for me!
They stab CAESAR.

CAESAR

Et tu, Brutè?—Then fall, Caesar.
Dies.

CINNA

Liberty! Freedom! Tyranny is dead!
Run hence, proclaim, cry it about the streets.

CASSIUS

80   Some to the common pulpits, and cry out,
"Liberty, freedom, and enfranchisement!"

---

74 *Olympus*   a mountain in Greece thought to be the home of the gods.

CAESAR
I could be persuaded, if I were a man like you.
If I myself could plead to persuade others, then prayers
     would persuade me.
60   But I am as unchanging as the North Star,
whose completely fixed and immovable nature
is unmatched by any other star in the heavens.
The skies are adorned with innumerable sparks of stars;
they are all made of fire and every one shines.
65   But there's only one among them all that keeps its position.
So it is in the world: it is well stocked with men,
and men are flesh and blood and capable of using their heads;
yet among them all I only know one
who cannot be tempted and keeps his position,
70   unmoved by any influences. And to show I am that man,
let me demonstrate it even in this small matter:
I was firm that Cimber should be banished,
and remain firm to keep him banished.

CINNA
O Caesar—

CAESAR
Away with you! Will you attempt the impossible, like lifting
     Mount Olympus?

DECIUS
Great Caesar—

CAESAR
75   Don't you see Brutus kneeling in vain?

CASCA
Let my hands speak for me!
          They stab CAESAR.

CAESAR
And thou also, Brutus? Then it is time for Caesar to fall.
          Dies.

CINNA
Liberty! Freedom! Tyranny is dead!
Run from here, proclaim, cry it about the streets.

CASSIUS
80   Let some go to the public speaking-platforms and cry out,
"Liberty, freedom, and the end of slavery!"

BRUTUS
People and senators, be not affrighted.
Fly not; stand still. Ambition's debt is paid.

CASCA
Go to the pulpit, Brutus.

DECIUS
85   And Cassius too.

BRUTUS
Where's Publius?

CINNA
Here, quite confounded with this mutiny.

METELLUS
Stand fast together, lest some friend of Caesar's
Should chance—

BRUTUS
90   Talk not of standing. Publius, good cheer,
There is no harm intended to your person,
Nor to no Roman else. So tell them, Publius.

CASSIUS
And leave us, Publius, lest that the people,
Rushing on us, should do your age some mischief.

BRUTUS
95   Do so; and let no man abide this deed
But we the doers.

Enter TREBONIUS.

CASSIUS
Where is Antony?

TREBONIUS
Fled to his house amazed.
Men, wives, and children stare, cry out, and run,
As it were doomsday.

BRUTUS
Fates,* we will know your pleasures.
100   That we shall die, we know; 'tis but the time,
And drawing days out, that men stand upon.

CASCA
Why, he that cuts off twenty years of life
Cuts off so many years of fearing death.

---

99   *Fates*   see note at 2.3.13.

BRUTUS

People and senators, don't be frightened.
Don't run away ; stand still. Caesar's ambition has received
  its just reward.

CASCA

Go to the speaking-platform, Brutus.

DECIUS

85 And Cassius too.

BRUTUS

Where's Publius?

CINNA

Here, quite stunned by this rebellion.

METELLUS

Let's all keep together and prepare to defend ourselves,
  if some friend of Caesar's
should happen—

BRUTUS

90 Don't talk about making a stand. Publius, be cheerful,
there is no harm intended to you
or to any other Roman. Tell everybody that, Publius.

CASSIUS

And leave us, Publius, in case the people,
rushing on us in their joy, might do your old age some injury.

BRUTUS

95 Do so, and let no one be responsible for this deed
except us, the doers.
  Enter TREBONIUS.

CASSIUS

Where is Antony?

TREBONIUS

Fled to his house, astounded.
Men, wives, and children stare, cry out, and run about
as if it were Judgment Day.

BRUTUS

Fates, we want to know your intentions.
100 We know that we will die eventually—it's only the exact time
and the prolonging of life that men consider significant.

CASCA

Why, he that cuts off twenty years of life
cuts off that many years of fearing death.

BRUTUS

Grant that, and then is death a benefit.
105 So are we Caesar's friends, that have abridged
His time of fearing death. Stoop, Romans, stoop,
And let us bathe our hands in Caesar's blood
Up to the elbows, and besmear our swords.
Then walk we forth, even to the market place,
110 And waving our red weapons o'er our heads,
Let's all cry, "Peace, freedom, and liberty!"

CASSIUS

Stoop then, and wash. How many ages hence
Shall this our lofty scene be acted over,
In states unborn and accents yet unknown!

BRUTUS

115 How many times shall Caesar bleed in sport,
That now on Pompey's basis lies along
No worthier than the dust!

CASSIUS

So oft as that shall be,
So often shall the knot of us be called
The men that gave their country liberty.

DECIUS

What, shall we forth?

CASSIUS

120 Ay, every man away.
Brutus shall lead, and we will grace his heels
With the most boldest and best hearts of Rome.
Enter a Servant.

BRUTUS

Soft, who comes here? A friend of Antony's.

SERVANT

Thus, Brutus, did my master bid me kneel;
125 Thus did Mark Antony bid me fall down;
And being prostrate, thus he bade me say:
Brutus is noble, wise, valiant, and honest;
Caesar was mighty, bold, royal, and loving.
Say, I love Brutus and I honor him;

BRUTUS

Agree to that, and then death becomes a benefit.
Thus we are Caesar's friends, who have shortened
his time of fearing death. Stoop, Romans, stoop,
and let us bathe our hands in Caesar's blood
up to the elbows, and smear our swords with it.
Then let us walk out as far as the market place,
and waving our red weapons over our heads,
let's all cry, "Peace, freedom, and liberty!"

CASSIUS

Stoop then and wash your hands. How many ages from now
shall our noble scene be acted once again,
in countries that don't yet exist and in languages still unknown!

BRUTUS

How many times shall Caesar bleed in a play,
who now lies stretched out on the pedestal of Pompey's statue
no better than the dust in which he lies!

CASSIUS

As often as that happens,
our little band will be called
the men who gave their country liberty.

DECIUS

Shall we leave the Capitol?

CASSIUS

Yes, let every man depart.
Brutus shall lead the way, and we will follow him, doing
honor to the very heels of his feet,
with the boldest and best spirits in Rome.
Enter a Servant.

BRUTUS

Wait a minute, who comes here? It's a friend of Antony's.

SERVANT

Thus, Brutus, my master ordered me to kneel to you;
thus Mark Antony ordered me to fall down at your feet,
and being prone, thus he ordered me to speak:
Brutus is noble, wise, brave, and honest;
Caesar was mighty, bold, royal, and loving.
Say, I love Brutus and I honor him;

130 Say, I feared Caesar, honored him, and loved him.
If Brutus will vouchsafe that Antony
May safely come to him, and be resolved
How Caesar hath deserved to lie in death,
Mark Antony shall not love Caesar dead
135 So well as Brutus living; but will follow
The fortunes and affairs of noble Brutus
Thorough the hazards of this untrod state
With all true faith. So says my master Antony.

BRUTUS
Thy master is a wise and valiant Roman;
140 I never thought him worse.
Tell him, so please him come unto this place,
He shall be satisfied; and by my honor
Depart untouched.

SERVANT
                    I'll fetch him presently.
        Exit Servant.

BRUTUS
I know that we shall have him well to friend.

CASSIUS
145 I wish we may. But yet have I a mind
That fears him much; and my misgiving still
Falls shrewdly to the purpose.
        Enter ANTONY.

BRUTUS
But here comes Antony. Welcome, Mark Antony.

ANTONY
O mighty Caesar! Dost thou lie so low?
150 Are all thy conquests, glories, triumphs, spoils,
Shrunk to this little measure? Fare thee well.
I know not, gentlemen, what you intend,
Who else must be let blood, who else is rank.
If I myself, there is no hour so fit
155 As Caesar's death's hour; nor no instrument
Of half that worth as those your swords, made rich
With the most noble blood of all this world.

130   Say, I feared Caesar, honored him, and loved him.
       If Brutus will guarantee that Antony
       may safely come to him and be informed
       why Caesar deserved to die,
       Mark Antony shall not love the dead Caesar
       so well as the living Brutus. And, with all true faith, he will
135   take his part in
       the fortunes and undertakings of noble Brutus
       through all the difficulties of this new and uncertain state
           of affairs.
       So says my master Antony.

BRUTUS
       Your master is a wise and brave Roman—
140   I never considered him any worse than that.
       Tell him, if he would kindly come to this place,
       he shall be fully informed, and, by my honor,
       leave here without any harm.

SERVANT
       I'll get him at once.
               Exit Servant.

BRUTUS
       I know that we shall have Antony as our friend.

CASSIUS
145   I hope we may. But when I think about it
       I fear him greatly, and my misgivings always
       turn out to be unpleasantly near the truth.
               Enter ANTONY.

BRUTUS
       But here comes Antony. Welcome, Mark Antony.

ANTONY   (*addressing the dead Caesar*)
       O mighty Caesar! Do you now lie so low?
150   Are all your conquests, glories, triumphs, spoils of war,
       shrunk to such a little size? Farewell.
       (*Addressing the conspirators*) I do not know, gentlemen,
           what your intentions are,
       who else's blood must be spilled, who else you consider corrupt.
       If I myself, there is no time so suitable
155   as the hour of Caesar's death, and no instrument
       of half the value as your swords, enriched
       with the most noble blood of all this world.

I do beseech ye, if you bear me hard,
Now, whilst your purpled hands do reek and smoke,
160   Fulfill your pleasure. Live a thousand years,
I shall not find myself so apt to die.
No place will please me so, no mean of death,
As here by Caesar, and by you cut off,
The choice and master spirits of this age.

BRUTUS
165   O Antony! Beg not your death of us.
Though now we must appear bloody and cruel,
As by our hands and this our present act
You see we do; yet see you but our hands,
And this the bleeding business they have done.
170   Our hearts you see not; they are pitiful;
And pity to the general wrong of Rome—
As fire drives out fire, so pity pity—*
Hath done this deed on Caesar. For your part,
To you our swords have leaden points, Mark Antony.
175   Our arms in strength of malice, and our hearts
Of brothers' temper, do receive you in
With all kind love, good thoughts, and reverence.

CASSIUS
Your voice shall be as strong as any man's
In the disposing of new dignities.

BRUTUS
180   Only be patient till we have appeased
The multitude, beside themselves with fear,
And then we will deliver you the cause
Why I, that did love Caesar when I struck him,
Have thus proceeded.

ANTONY
                        I doubt not of your wisdom.
185   Let each man render me his bloody hand.
First, Marcus Brutus, will I shake with you;
Next, Caius Cassius, do I take your hand;
Now, Decius Brutus, yours; now yours, Metellus;
Yours, Cinna; and, my valiant Casca, yours.

---

172 *As fire . . . pity* proverbial formulas. "Pity to the general wrong of
Rome" has driven out pity for Caesar, who was the cause of Rome's plight

I beg of you, if you have a grudge against me,
now, while your crimsoned hands steam with Caesar's blood,
60   satisfy your will. If I lived a thousand years,
I would never find myself so ready to die.
No place will please me so much, no means of death,
as here by Caesar and by you to be cut off—
the leading and strongest spirits of this age.

BRUTUS

65   O Antony! Don't beg your death from our hands.
Though now we must appear bloody and cruel,
as you can see by our hands and by this assassination of ours;
yet you only see our hands,
and the bloody business they have done.
70   You don't see our hearts—they are full of pity,
and pity for the wrongs that Romans have suffered—
as fire fights fire, so one kind of pity drives out another—
has done this deed to Caesar. As for you,
to you our swords have blunted, harmless points, Mark Antony.
With our arms, which must seem to you steeped in evil,
75   and with our hearts,
full of brotherly affection, we receive you as one of us,
with all kind love, good thoughts, and respect.

CASSIUS

Your opinion will count as much as anyone's
in making appointments to the new offices of state.

BRUTUS

80   Only be patient until we have quieted down
the Roman people, who are now beside themselves with fear,
and then we will explain to you the reason
why I, who loved Caesar even when I struck him,
have acted in this way.

ANTONY

I do not doubt your wisdom.
85   Let each man give me his bloody hand.
First, Marcus Brutus, will I shake with you;
next, Caius Cassius, I take your hand;
now, Decius Brutus, yours; now yours, Metellus;
yours, Cinna; and, my valiant Casca, yours.

190   Though last, not least in love, yours, good Trebonius.
    Gentlemen all—alas, what shall I say?
    My credit now stands on such slippery ground
    That one of two bad ways you must conceit me,
    Either a coward or a flatterer.
195   That I did love thee, Caesar, O 'tis true.
    If then thy spirit look upon us now,
    Shall it not grieve thee dearer than thy death
    To see thy Antony making his peace,
    Shaking the bloody fingers of thy foes,
200   Most noble, in the presence of thy corse?
    Had I as many eyes as thou hast wounds,
    Weeping as fast as they stream forth thy blood,
    It would become me better than to close
    In terms of friendship with thine enemies.
205   Pardon me, Julius! Here wast thou bayed, brave hart;*
    Here didst thou fall; and here thy hunters stand,
    Signed in thy spoil, and crimsoned in thy lethe.
    O world, thou wast the forest to this hart,
    And this indeed, O world, the heart of thee!
210   How like a deer, strucken by many princes,
    Dost thou here lie!

CASSIUS
    Mark Antony—

ANTONY
                    Pardon me, Caius Cassius.
    The enemies of Caesar shall say this;
    Then, in a friend, it is cold modesty.

CASSIUS
215   I blame you not for praising Caesar so,
    But what compact mean you to have with us?
    Will you be pricked* in number of our friends,
    Or shall we on, and not depend on you?

ANTONY
    Therefore I took your hands, but was indeed
220   Swayed from the point by looking down on Caesar.

---

205 *hart*   wordplay on "hart-heart." "Hart" is the adult male deer, usually
the red deer.

190   Though last, not least in love, yours, good Trebonius.
     Gentlemen all—alas, what shall I say?
     My credibility is now so uncertain
     that you must think of me in one of two bad ways:
     either a coward or a flatterer.
195   That I loved you, Caesar, O it's true.
     If then your spirit looks upon us now,
     shall it not grieve you more keenly than your death
     to see your Antony making his peace,
     shaking the bloody fingers of your enemies,
200   most noble Caesar, in the very presence of your corpse?
     Had I as many eyes as you have wounds,
     weeping as fast as the blood flows out of those wounds—
     to weep would be more appropriate than to make
     a friendly pact with your enemies.
     Pardon me, Julius! Here is where you were cornered,
205   brave heart,
     here you fell, and here your hunters stand,
     marked with your slaughter and crimsoned with your lifeblood.
     O world, you were the forest to this deer,
     and this indeed, O world, was your dear one!
210   How like a deer, struck down by many princes,
     do you lie here!

CASSIUS
     Mark Antony—

ANTONY
     Pardon me, Caius Cassius.
     Even the enemies of Caesar shall say as much;
     then, for a friend, it is only a cold and moderate way of talking.

CASSIUS
215   I don't blame you for praising Caesar this way,
     but what sort of agreement do you mean to have with us?
     Will you be counted in the list of our friends,
     or shall we proceed and not depend on you?

ANTONY
     That's why I took your hands, but was indeed
220   distracted from the issue by looking down on Caesar's body.

---

217 *pricked*   marked down, by making a pinhole or dot next to the name
on a list.

Friends am I with you all, and love you all,
Upon this hope, that you shall give me reasons
Why and wherein Caesar was dangerous.

BRUTUS

Or else were this a savage spectacle.
225   Our reasons are so full of good regard
That were you, Antony, the son of Caesar,
You should be satisfied.

ANTONY

               That's all I seek,
And am moreover suitor that I may
Produce his body to the market place,
230   And in the pulpit, as becomes a friend,
Speak in the order of his funeral.

BRUTUS

You shall, Mark Antony.

CASSIUS

              Brutus, a word with you.
[*Aside to Brutus*] You know not what you do. Do not
    consent
That Antony speak in his funeral.
235   Know you how much the people may be moved
By that which he will utter?

BRUTUS

[*Aside to Cassius*]   By your pardon—
I will myself into the pulpit first,
And show the reason of our Caesar's death.
What Antony shall speak, I will protest
240   He speaks by leave and by permission;
And that we are contented Caesar shall
Have all true rites and lawful ceremonies,
It shall advantage more than do us wrong.

CASSIUS

[*Aside to Brutus*] I know not what may fall; I like it not.

BRUTUS

245   Mark Antony, here, take you Caesar's body.
You shall not in your funeral speech blame us,

I am friends with you all and love you all,
with this hope, that you shall give me reasons
why and how Caesar was dangerous.

BRUTUS
If we couldn't do that, this murder would be a savage spectacle.
225 Our reasons are so good and so persuasive
that were you, Antony, the son of Caesar,
you would be satisfied.

ANTONY
That's all I seek,
and I also request that I may
take Caesar's body to the market place,
230 and from the speaker's platform, as befits a friend,
speak at Caesar's funeral ceremony.

BRUTUS
You shall, Mark Antony.

CASSIUS
Brutus, let me have a word with you.
(*To Brutus*) You don't know what you are doing. Do not consent
to let Antony speak at Caesar's funeral.
235 Do you realize how much the people may be moved
by what Antony will say?

BRUTUS (*to Cassius*)
Pardon me,
but I will go up to the speaker's platform first
and explain the reasons for our Caesar's death.
What Antony will speak, I will proclaim
240 is spoken only by our leave and our permission.
The fact that we want Caesar
to have all the proper rites and lawful ceremonies
will benefit rather than harm us.

CASSIUS (*to Brutus*)
I don't know what may happen, but I don't like this.

BRUTUS
245 Mark Antony, here, take Caesar's body.
You shall not in your funeral speech blame us,

But speak all good you can devise of Caesar,
And say you do't by our permission.
Else shall you not have any hand at all
250   About his funeral. And you shall speak
In the same pulpit whereto I am going,
After my speech is ended.

ANTONY

                         Be it so;
I do desire no more.

BRUTUS

Prepare the body then, and follow us.
            Exeunt. ANTONY *remains.*

ANTONY

255   O pardon me, thou bleeding piece of earth,
That I am meek and gentle with these butchers.
Thou art the ruins of the noblest man
That ever livèd in the tide of times.
Woe to the hand that shed this costly blood!
260   Over thy wounds now do I prophesy
(Which like dumb mouths do ope their ruby lips
To beg the voice and utterance of my tongue),
A curse shall light upon the limbs of men;
Domestic fury and fierce civil strife
265   Shall cumber all the parts of Italy;
Blood and destruction shall be so in use,
And dreadful objects so familiar,
That mothers shall but smile when they behold
Their infants quartered with the hands of war,
270   All pity choked with custom of fell deeds;
And Caesar's spirit, ranging for revenge,
With Até* by his side come hot from hell,
Shall in these confines with a monarch's voice
Cry "Havoc!" and let slip the dogs of war,
275   That this foul deed shall smell above the earth
With carrion men, groaning for burial.
            Enter Octavio's Servant.
You serve Octavius Caesar, do you not?

---

272 *Até* Greek goddess of discord and vengeance.

but speak all the good you can think of about Caesar,
and say you do it only by our permission.
Otherwise you won't have any hand at all
250   in Caesar's funeral. And you shall speak
from the same platform where I am going,
after my speech is over.

ANTONY
    So be it;
    I desire nothing more.

BRUTUS
    Prepare the body then and follow us.
       All exit except ANTONY.

ANTONY *(addressing Caesar's body)*
255   O pardon me, you bleeding piece of mortal earth,
that I am meek and gentle with these butchers.
You are the ruins of the noblest man
that ever lived in the course of history.
I warn those who have shed this costly blood that they will
    pay for it!
260   Over your wounds I now foretell the future—
those wounds which, like silent mouths, open their ruby lips
to beg me to speak for them—
a curse shall fall on everything that men do.
Family strife and fierce civil war
265   shall oppress all parts of Italy.
Blood and destruction shall be so common,
and fearful sights so familiar,
that mothers will only smile when they behold
their infants chopped in pieces by the hands of war—
270   all their pity choked by the commoness of such savage acts.
And the spirit of Caesar, hunting for revenge,
with Até by his side coming hot from hell,
in this region with a monarch's voice will
cry out for unlimited slaughter and unleash the dogs of war,
275   so that this vile murder shall smell above the earth
with decaying bodies, groaning to be buried.
       Enter Octavio's Servant.
You serve Octavius Caesar, do you not?

SERVANT
I do, Mark Antony.
ANTONY
Caesar did write for him to come to Rome.
SERVANT
280   He did receive his letters and is coming,
And bid me say to you by word of mouth—
O Caesar!
ANTONY
Thy heart is big; get thee apart and weep.
Passion I see is catching, for mine eyes,
285   Seeing those beads of sorrow stand in thine,
Began to water. Is thy master coming?
SERVANT
He lies tonight within seven leagues of Rome.
ANTONY
Post back with speed, and tell him what hath chanced.
Here is a mourning Rome, a dangerous Rome,
290   No Rome* of safety for Octavius yet;
Hie hence and tell him so. Yet stay awhile;
Thou shalt not back till I have borne this corse
Into the market place. There shall I try,
In my oration, how the people take
295   The cruel issue of these bloody men;
According to the which thou shalt discourse
To young Octavius of the state of things.
Lend me your hand.
            Exeunt [with Caesar's body].

[*Scene ii: Rome, the Forum.*] *Enter* BRUTUS *and* CASSIUS, *with the Plebeians.*

PLEBEIANS
We will be satisfied. Let us be satisfied.
BRUTUS
Then follow me, and give me audience, friends.
Cassius, go you into the other street,
And part the numbers.
5   Those that will hear me speak, let 'em stay here;

---

290 *Rome* wordplay on "Rome-room." See note at 1.2.157.

SERVANT
I do, Mark Antony.

ANTONY
Julius Caesar wrote him to come to Rome.

SERVANT
280 Octavius received his letter and is coming,
and he ordered me to tell you by word of mouth—
(*breaks off with emotion*) O Caesar!

ANTONY
Your heart is full of grief; go aside and weep.
Sorrow I see is catching, because my eyes,
285 seeing those tears of sorrow in yours, also
began to weep. Is your master coming?

SERVANT
He lodges tonight about twenty miles from Rome.

ANTONY
Ride back with speed and tell him what has happened.
Here is a mourning Rome, a dangerous Rome,
290 no Rome to which Octavius can yet safely come.
Hurry there and tell him so. But wait a moment.
You shall not go back until I have taken Caesar's body
into the market place. There I shall test,
in my oration, how the people react to
295 the cruel outcome of these bloody conspirators.
According to the success of my speech, you shall inform
young Octavius how things stand in Rome.
Lend me a hand.
They exit, carrying out Caesar's body.

Scene ii: The Roman Forum. Enter BRUTUS *and* CASSIUS *with
a mob of ordinary Roman citizens.*

CITIZENS
We insist on a full explanation. Let us be properly informed.

BRUTUS
Then follow me and listen to me, friends.
Cassius, go into the other street
and divide the crowd.
5 Those that wish to hear me speak, let them stay here.

Those that will follow Cassius, go with him;
And public reasons shall be renderèd
Of Caesar's death.

FIRST PLEBEIAN

I will hear Brutus speak.

SECOND PLEBEIAN

I will hear Cassius, and compare their reasons
10   When severally we hear them renderèd.
[*Exit* CASSIUS, *with some of the Plebeians.*] BRUTUS *goes into the
pulpit.*

THIRD PLEBEIAN

The noble Brutus is ascended. Silence!

BRUTUS

Be patient till the last.
Romans, countrymen, and lovers, hear me for my cause, and be
silent, that you may hear. Believe me for mine honor, and have
15   respect to mine honor, that you may believe. Censure me in your
wisdom, and awake your senses, that you may the better judge.
If there be any in this assembly, any dear friend of Caesar's, to
him I say that Brutus' love to Caesar was no less than his. If then
that friend demand why Brutus rose against Caesar, this is my
20   answer: not that I loved Caesar less, but that I loved Rome more.
Had you rather Caesar were living, and die all slaves, than that
Caesar were dead, to live all freemen? As Caesar loved me, I
weep for him; as he was fortunate, I rejoice at it; as he was
valiant, I honor him; but, as he was ambitious, I slew him. There
25   is tears for his love; joy for his fortune; honor for his valor; and
death for his ambition. Who is here so base that would be a
bondman? If any, speak; for him have I offended. Who is here
so rude that would not be a Roman? If any, speak; for him have
I offended. Who is here so vile that will not love his country? If
30   any, speak; for him have I offended. I pause for a reply.

Those that wish to follow Cassius, go with him,
and an official account will be given
of Caesar's death.

FIRST CITIZEN
I will hear Brutus speak.

SECOND CITIZEN
I will hear Cassius, and compare their reasons
10   after we have heard them separately.

    Exit CASSIUS *with some of the citizens.* BRUTUS *goes
    up onto the speaking-platform.*

THIRD CITIZEN
The noble Brutus has mounted the platform. Silence!

BRUTUS
Be patient until the end of my speech.
Romans, countrymen, and dear friends: hear me for the sake
    of my cause, and be
15   silent that you may hear. Believe me for the sake of my honor, and
respect my honor that you may believe. Judge me in your
wisdom, and awaken your good sense that you may judge better.
If there is anyone in this crowd, any dear friend of Caesar's, to
him I say that Brutus's love of Caesar was no less than his.
    If then
that friend wants to know why Brutus rose up against
    Caesar, this is my
20   answer: not that I loved Caesar less, but that I loved Rome more.
Would you rather that Caesar were living and you all die
    as slaves, than that
Caesar were dead so that you all might live as free men?
    As Caesar loved me, I
weep for him; as he had good fortune, I rejoice at it; as he was
valiant, I honor him; but, as he was ambitious,
    I killed him. There
are tears for his love; joy for his good fortune; honor for
25   his valor; and
death for his ambition. Who is here so low that would be a
slave? If any, speak; for him have I done wrong. Who is here
so uncivilized that would not be a Roman? If any, speak;
    for him have
I done wrong. Who is here so vile that will not love
    his country? If
30   any, speak; for him have I done wrong. I pause for a reply.

ALL
None, Brutus, none.

BRUTUS
Then none have I offended. I have done no more to Caesar than
you shall do to Brutus. The question of his death is enrolled in
the Capitol; his glory not extenuated, wherein he was worthy;
35   nor his offenses enforced, for which he suffered death.

Enter MARK ANTONY, *with Caesar's body.*

Here comes his body, mourned by Mark Antony, who, though he
had no hand in his death, shall receive the benefit of his dying, a
place in the commonwealth, as which of you shall not? With this
I depart, that, as I slew my best lover for the good of Rome, I
40   have the same dagger for myself when it shall please my country
to need my death.

ALL
Live, Brutus! live, live!

FIRST PLEBEIAN
Bring him with triumph home unto his house.

SECOND PLEBEIAN
Give him a statue with his ancestors.

THIRD PLEBEIAN
Let him be Caesar.

FOURTH PLEBEIAN
45   Caesar's better parts
Shall be crowned in Brutus.

FIRST PLEBEIAN
We'll bring him to his house with shouts and clamors.

BRUTUS
My countrymen—

SECOND PLEBEIAN
                    Peace! Silence! Brutus speaks.

FIRST PLEBEIAN
Peace, ho!

BRUTUS
50   Good countrymen, let me depart alone,
And, for my sake, stay here with Antony.

ALL
  None, Brutus, none.
BRUTUS
  Then have I done wrong to no one. I have done no more
      to Caesar than
  you shall do to Brutus. The whole history of his death
      is recorded in
  the Capitol; his glory not undervalued, in which he was worthy;
35 nor his offenses emphasized, for which he suffered death.
      Enter MARK ANTONY *with Caesar's body.*
  Here comes his body, mourned by Mark Antony, who, though he
  had no hand in his death, shall benefit from his dying with a
  position in the new government—as which of you shall not?
      With these words
  I depart, that, as I killed my best friend for the good of Rome, I
  have the same dagger for myself when it shall please
40   my country
  to need my death.
ALL
  Live, Brutus! live, live!
FIRST CITIZEN
  Accompany him home with a victory procession.
SECOND CITIZEN
  Let us erect a statue for him alongside his ancestors.
THIRD CITIZEN
  Let him be Caesar.
FOURTH CITIZEN
45   Caesar's virtues
  shall be crowned in Brutus.
FIRST CITIZEN
  We'll accompany him to his house with shouts and clamors.
BRUTUS
  My countrymen—
SECOND CITIZEN
  Quiet! Silence! Brutus speaks.
FIRST CITIZEN
  Quiet there!
BRUTUS
0 Good countrymen, let me depart alone,
  and, for my sake, stay here with Antony.

Do grace to Caesar's corpse, and grace his speech
Tending to Caesar's glories, which Mark Antony,
By our permission, is allowed to make.

55   I do entreat you, not a man depart
Save I alone, till Antony have spoke.

       Exit.

FIRST PLEBEIAN
Stay, ho! and let us hear Mark Antony.

THIRD PLEBEIAN
Let him go up into the public chair;
We'll hear him. Noble Antony, go up.

ANTONY
60   For Brutus' sake, I am beholding to you.

FOURTH PLEBEIAN
What does he say of Brutus?

THIRD PLEBEIAN
                   He says, for Brutus' sake
He finds himself beholding to us all.

FOURTH PLEBEIAN
'Twere best he speak no harm of Brutus here!

FIRST PLEBEIAN
This Caesar was a tyrant.

THIRD PLEBEIAN
                 Nay, that's certain.
65   We are blest that Rome is rid of him.

SECOND PLEBEIAN
Peace! Let us hear what Antony can say.

ANTONY
You gentle Romans—

ALL
             Peace, ho! Let us hear him.

ANTONY
Friends, Romans, countrymen, lend me your ears;
I come to bury Caesar, not to praise him.
70   The evil that men do lives after them,
The good is oft interrèd with their bones;
So let it be with Caesar. The noble Brutus
Hath told you Caesar was ambitious.

Pay your respects to Caesar's corpse, and honor his speech
about Caesar's glories, which Mark Antony,
with our permission, is allowed to make.
55   I beg of you, don't let anyone leave
(except me) until Antony has spoken.
    Exit.

FIRST CITIZEN
Wait there! and let us hear Mark Antony.

THIRD CITIZEN
Let him go up to the public platform;
we'll hear him. Noble Antony, go up.

ANTONY
60   For Brutus's sake, I am obliged to you.

FOURTH CITIZEN
What does he say of Brutus?

THIRD CITIZEN
He says for Brutus's sake
he finds himself obliged to us all.

FOURTH CITIZEN
It would be best for him if he didn't speak any harm
    of Brutus here!

FIRST CITIZEN
This Caesar was a tyrant.

THIRD CITIZEN
Indeed, that's certain.
65   We are blest that Rome is rid of him.

SECOND CITIZEN
Quiet! Let us hear what Antony can say.

ANTONY
You gentle Romans—

ALL
Quiet, there! Let us hear him.

ANTONY
Friends, Romans, countrymen: listen to me.
I come to bury Caesar's body, not to make a speech praising him.
70   The evil men do is remembered after they're dead,
but the good is often buried with their bones.
Thus let it be with Caesar. The noble Brutus
has told you that Caesar was ambitious.

If it were so, it was a grievous fault,
75 And grievously hath Caesar answered it.
Here, under leave of Brutus and the rest—
For Brutus is an honorable man;
So are they all, all honorable men—
Come I to speak in Caesar's funeral.
80 He was my friend, faithful and just to me;
But Brutus says he was ambitious,
And Brutus is an honorable man.
He hath brought many captives home to Rome,
Whose ransoms did the general coffers fill.
85 Did this in Caesar seem ambitious?
When that the poor have cried, Caesar hath wept.
Ambition should be made of sterner stuff,
Yet Brutus says he was ambitious;
And Brutus is an honorable man.
90 You all did see that on the Lupercal*
I thrice presented him a kingly crown,
Which he did thrice refuse. Was this ambition?
Yet Brutus says he was ambitious;
And sure he is an honorable man.
95 I speak not to disprove what Brutus spoke,
But here I am to speak what I do know.
You all did love him once, not without cause;
What cause withholds you then to mourn for him?
O judgment! Thou art fled to brutish beasts,
100 And men have lost their reason. Bear with me;
My heart is in the coffin there with Caesar,
And I must pause till it come back to me.

FIRST PLEBEIAN
Methinks there is much reason in his sayings.

SECOND PLEBEIAN
If thou consider rightly of the matter,
Caesar has had great wrong.

THIRD PLEBEIAN
                              Has he, masters?
105 I fear there will a worse come in his place.

---

90 *Lupercal*   see note at 1.1.66.

If it were true, it was a serious fault in him,
and Caesar has paid for it most dearly.
Here, with the permission of Brutus and his friends—
for Brutus is an honorable man;
so are all his friends, all honorable men—
I come to speak at Caesar's funeral.
He was my friend, faithful and true to me;
but Brutus says he was ambitious,
and Brutus is an honorable man.
Caesar brought many prisoners of war home to Rome,
whose ransoms filled the public treasury.
Did this action of Caesar seem ambitious?
When poor people cried, Caesar wept with them—
ambition should be more unfeeling than that,
yet Brutus says that Caesar was ambitious,
and Brutus is an honorable man.
You all saw that on the day of the Lupercalian festival
I presented him with a kingly crown three times,
which he refused three times. Was this ambition?
Yet Brutus says that Caesar was ambitious,
and surely Brutus is an honorable man.
I am not speaking to disprove what Brutus spoke,
but I am here to speak what I myself know.
Everyone loved Caesar once, not without good reason;
what reason then keeps you from mourning for him?
O good sense! you have fled to savage beasts
and men have lost their powers of reason. Bear with me;
my own heart is in the coffin there with Caesar's body,
and I have to pause until it returns to me.

FIRST CITIZEN

I think there is much good sense in what he is saying.

SECOND CITIZEN

If you consider the matter properly,
great wrong has been done to Caesar.

THIRD CITIZEN

Has there been, comrades?
I fear that a worse ruler will come to take Caesar's place.

FOURTH PLEBEIAN
　　Marked ye his words? He would not take the crown;
　　Therefore 'tis certain he was not ambitious.
FIRST PLEBEIAN
　　If it be found so, some will dear abide it.
SECOND PLEBEIAN
110　　Poor soul, his eyes are red as fire with weeping.
THIRD PLEBEIAN
　　There's not a nobler man in Rome than Antony.
FOURTH PLEBEIAN
　　Now mark him, he begins again to speak.
ANTONY
　　But yesterday, the word of Caesar might
　　Have stood against the world. Now lies he there,
115　　And none so poor to do him reverence.
　　O masters! If I were disposed to stir
　　Your hearts and minds to mutiny and rage,
　　I should do Brutus wrong, and Cassius wrong,
　　Who, you all know, are honorable men.
120　　I will not do them wrong. I rather choose
　　To wrong the dead, to wrong myself and you,
　　Than I will wrong such honorable men.
　　But here's a parchment with the seal of Caesar;
　　I found it in his closet, 'tis his will.
125　　Let but the commons hear this testament,
　　Which, pardon me, I do not mean to read,
　　And they would go and kiss dead Caesar's wounds,
　　And dip their napkins in his sacred blood;
　　Yea, beg a hair of him for memory,
130　　And dying, mention it within their wills,
　　Bequeathing it as a rich legacy
　　Unto their issue.
FOURTH PLEBEIAN
　　We'll hear the will; read it, Mark Antony.
ALL
　　The will, the will! We will hear Caesar's will.
ANTONY
135　　Have patience, gentle friends; I must not read it.
　　It is not meet you know how Caesar loved you.

FOURTH CITIZEN
    Did you pay attention to Antony's words? Caesar didn't want
        to be crowned;
    Therefore it's certain he was not ambitious.
FIRST CITIZEN
    If that turns out to be true, some will pay dearly for it.
SECOND CITIZEN
10   Poor Antony, his eyes are red as fire with weeping.
THIRD CITIZEN
    There's not a nobler man in Rome than Antony.
FOURTH CITIZEN
    Now listen to him, he begins to speak again.
ANTONY
    Only yesterday, Caesar's word alone might
    have stood up against the whole world. Now he lies in his coffin,
    and there is no one, however humble, who dares pay him
15   all due respect.
    O gentlemen! If I were inclined to stir up
    your hearts and minds to mutiny and rage,
    I would be doing Brutus wrong, and Cassius wrong,
    who, you all know, are honorable men.
20   I will not do them wrong. I prefer
    to wrong the dead, to wrong myself and you,
    rather than wrong such honorable men.
    But here's a document with Caesar's seal on it.
    I found it in his study; it's his will.
25   If the common people could only hear this will
    (which, pardon me, I do not intend to read)
    they would go and kiss dead Caesar's wounds,
    and dip their handkerchiefs in his holy blood.
    They would even pluck out one of his hairs as a memorial,
30   and, when they died, mention it in their own wills,
    leaving it as a rich gift
    to their children.
FOURTH CITIZEN
    We'll hear the will; read it, Mark Antony.
ALL
    The will, the will! We will hear Caesar's will.
ANTONY
35   Be patient, gentle friends; I must not read it.
    It is not proper that you should know how much
        Caesar loved you.

You are not wood, you are not stones, but men;
And being men, hearing the will of Caesar,
It will inflame you, it will make you mad.
140 'Tis good you know not that you are his heirs,
For if you should, O what would come of it?
FOURTH PLEBEIAN
Read the will, we'll hear it, Antony.
You shall read us the will, Caesar's will.
ANTONY
Will you be patient? Will you stay awhile?
145 I have o'ershot myself to tell you of it.
I fear I wrong the honorable men
Whose daggers have stabbed Caesar; I do fear it.
FOURTH PLEBEIAN
They were traitors. Honorable men!
ALL
The will! The testament!
SECOND PLEBEIAN
150 They were villains, murderers. The will! Read the will!
ANTONY
You will compel me then to read the will?
Then make a ring about the corpse of Caesar,
And let me show you him that made the will.
Shall I descend? And will you give me leave?
ALL
155 Come down.
SECOND PLEBEIAN
Descend.
THIRD PLEBEIAN
You shall have leave.
FOURTH PLEBEIAN
A ring, stand round.
FIRST PLEBEIAN
Stand from the hearse, stand from the body.
SECOND PLEBEIAN
160 Room for Antony, most noble Antony.
ANTONY
Nay, press not so upon me; stand far off.
ALL
Stand back! Room! Bear back!

You are not wood, you are not stones, but human beings
   (and therefore capable of feelings),
and being men, when you hear the will of Caesar,
it will inflame you, it will make you mad.

140   It's good you don't know that you are Caesar's heirs,
because if you should know, O what might happen?

FOURTH CITIZEN
Read the will. We'll hear it, Antony.
You shall read us the will, Caesar's will.

ANTONY
Will you be patient? Will you remain here awhile?

145   I have gone further than I intended in telling you about it.
I fear that I wrong the honorable men
whose daggers have stabbed Caesar. I really fear it.

FOURTH CITIZEN
They were traitors. What do you mean, "honorable men"?

ALL
The will! The testament!

SECOND CITIZEN
150   They were villains, murderers. The will! Read the will!

ANTONY
You will force me then to read the will?
Then make a ring about the corpse of Caesar,
and let me show you the sort of man who made the will.
Shall I come down? And will you give me your permission?

ALL
155   Come down.

SECOND CITIZEN
Descend.

THIRD CITIZEN
You shall have permission.

FOURTH CITIZEN
Make a ring. Stand around.

FIRST CITIZEN
Stand away from the coffin, stand away from the body.

SECOND CITIZEN
160   Make room for Antony, most noble Antony.

ANTONY
Please, don't crowd me so closely. Stand a little further away.

ALL
Stand back! Make room! Move back!

ANTONY

If you have tears, prepare to shed them now.
You all do know this mantle. I remember

165   The first time ever Caesar put it on;
'Twas on a summer's evening in his tent,
That day he overcame the Nervii.*
Look, in this place ran Cassius' dagger through.
See what a rent the envious Casca made.

170   Through this the well-belovèd Brutus stabbed;
And as he plucked his cursèd steel away,
Mark how the blood of Caesar followed it,
As rushing out of doors to be resolved
If Brutus so unkindly knocked, or no;

175   For Brutus, as you know, was Caesar's angel.
Judge, O you gods, how dearly Caesar loved him.
This was the most unkindest cut of all;
For when the noble Caesar saw him stab,
Ingratitude, more strong than traitors' arms,

180   Quite vanquished him. Then burst his mighty heart,
And in his mantle muffling up his face,
Even at the base of Pompey's statue,
Which all the while ran blood,* great Caesar fell.
O what a fall was there, my countrymen!

185   Then I, and you, and all of us fell down,
Whilst bloody treason flourished over us.
O now you weep, and I perceive you feel
The dint of pity. These are gracious drops.
Kind souls, what weep you when you but behold

190   Our Caesar's vesture wounded? Look you here,
Here is himself, marred as you see with traitors.

FIRST PLEBEIAN

O piteous spectacle!

SECOND PLEBEIAN

O noble Caesar!

THIRD PLEBEIAN

O woeful day!

FOURTH PLEBEIAN

195   O traitors, villains!

---

167 *Nervii* a fierce tribe of Gaul conquered by Caesar in 57 B.C. at the
battle of the Sambre, one of his most decisive victories.
183 *ran blood* in popular belief, the corpse of a murdered man (here

ANTONY

 If you are capable of tears, prepare to weep them now.
 You all recognize this cloak. I remember
165 the first time that Caesar ever put it on.
 It was on a summer evening in his tent,
 that day he defeated the Nervii.
 Look, in this place Cassius's dagger made a hole.
 See what a rip the malicious Casca made.
170 Through this spot the well-beloved Brutus stabbed,
 and as he pulled out the cursed steel,
 notice how the blood of Caesar followed it,
 as if it were rushing out to be sure
 whether or not Brutus knocked so cruelly on the door—
175 because Brutus, as you know, was Caesar's best friend.
 Judge, O you gods, how dearly Caesar loved him (and how
  costly it was to Caesar to have such a friend).
 Brutus's blow was the cruellest and most unnatural wound of all,
 because when the noble Caesar saw him stab,
 the thought of Brutus's ingratitude, stronger even than the
  weapons of traitors,
180 completely vanquished Caesar. Then his mighty heart burst,
 and covering up his face in his cloak, great Caesar fell
 at the pedestal of Pompey's statue
 (which bled all during the stabbing).
 O what a fall there was, my countrymen!
185 Then I, and you, and all of us fell down,
 while bloody treason lorded it over us.
 O now you weep, and I see that you feel
 the force of pity. These tears show your compassion.
 Kind souls, how you weep when you only behold
190 the wounds in Caesar's garment. Look here (*pulls off*
  Caesar's bloody cloak)—
 here is Caesar himself, his body mangled, as you see, by traitors.

FIRST CITIZEN

 O pitiful spectacle!

SECOND CITIZEN

 O noble Caesar!

THIRD CITIZEN

 O terrible day!

FOURTH CITIZEN

195 O traitors, villains!

Pompey's statue) bleeds in the presence of his murderer (Caesar). It seems
more likely that Antony means that Pompey's statue is bleeding in sympathetic outrage at the murder of Caesar.

FIRST PLEBEIAN
O most bloody sight!

SECOND PLEBEIAN
We will be revenged.

ALL
Revenge! About! Seek! Burn! Fire! Kill! Slay!
Let not a traitor live!

ANTONY
200   Stay, countrymen.

FIRST PLEBEIAN
Peace there! Hear the noble Antony.

SECOND PLEBEIAN
We'll hear him, we'll follow him, we'll die with him

ANTONY
Good friends, sweet friends, let me not stir you up
To such a sudden flood of mutiny.
205   They that have done this deed are honorable.
What private griefs they have, alas, I know not,
That made them do it. They are wise and honorable,
And will no doubt with reasons answer you.
I come not, friends, to steal away your hearts;
210   I am no orator, as Brutus is,
But, as you know me all, a plain blunt man
That love my friend; and that they know full well
That gave me public leave to speak of him.
For I have neither wit, nor words, nor worth,
215   Action, nor utterance, nor the power of speech
To stir men's blood. I only speak right on.
I tell you that which you yourselves do know,
Show you sweet Caesar's wounds, poor poor dumb mouths,
And bid them speak for me. But were I Brutus,
220   And Brutus Antony, there were an Antony
Would ruffle up your spirits, and put a tongue
In every wound of Caesar, that should move
The stones of Rome to rise and mutiny.

FIRST CITIZEN

O most bloody sight!

SECOND CITIZEN

We will be revenged.

ALL

Revenge! Let's be off! Seek out the conspirators! Burn! Set fires! Kill! Slay!

Don't let a single traitor live!

ANTONY

Wait, countrymen.

FIRST CITIZEN

Quiet there! Hear the noble Antony.

SECOND CITIZEN

We'll hear him, we'll follow him, we'll die with him.

ANTONY

Good friends, sweet friends, don't let me stir you up to such a sudden outpouring of mutiny.

Those who have done this deed are honorable.

What private grudges they have that made them do it, alas, I don't know.

They are wise and honorable,

and will no doubt be able to explain themselves with the proper reasons.

I don't come here, friends, to arouse your strong feelings.

I'm not a public speaker, as Brutus is,

but, as you all know me, only a plain, blunt man

who loves his friend Caesar. And they know that too,

those who gave me permission to speak in public about Caesar.

Because I have neither the intelligence, the eloquence, the reputation,

the knowledge of gesture, the proper delivery, nor the power of speech

to stir up men's passions. I only know how to speak directly.

I only tell you things that you yourselves know,

show you sweet Caesar's wounds (poor silent mouths)

and ask them to speak for me. But if I were Brutus

and Brutus were Antony, then there would be an Antony

who would know how to enrage your spirits, and who could put a tongue

in every wound of Caesar that would speak so movingly that the very stones of Rome would rise up and mutiny.

ALL
> We'll mutiny.

FIRST PLEBEIAN
> > We'll burn the house of Brutus.

THIRD PLEBEIAN
> Away, then; come, seek the conspirators.

ANTONY
> Yet hear me, countrymen; yet hear me speak.

ALL
> Peace, ho! Hear Antony, most noble Antony.

ANTONY
> Why, friends, you go to do you know not what.
> Wherein hath Caesar thus deserved your loves?
> Alas, you know not; I must tell you then.
> You have forgot the will I told you of.

ALL
> Most true, the will; let's stay and hear the will.

ANTONY
> Here is the will, and under Caesar's seal.
> To every Roman citizen he gives,
> To every several man, seventy-five drachmas.*

SECOND PLEBEIAN
> Most noble Caesar, we'll revenge his death.

THIRD PLEBEIAN
> O royal Caesar!

ANTONY
> Hear me with patience.

ALL
> Peace, ho!

ANTONY
> Moreover, he hath left you all his walks,
> His private arbors, and new-planted orchards,
> On this side Tiber; he hath left them you,
> And to your heirs for ever: common pleasures,
> To walk abroad and recreate yourselves.
> Here was a Caesar! When comes such another?

---

235 *seventy-five drachmas* The drachma was an ancient Greek silve
coin, whose English value (about ten pence) would not be generally know

ALL
  We'll mutiny.

FIRST CITIZEN
  We'll burn the house of Brutus.

THIRD CITIZEN
225 Away, then. Come, let's seek the conspirators.

ANTONY
  Still listen to me, countrymen; still listen to me speak.

ALL
  Quiet there! Hear Antony, most noble Antony.

ANTONY
  Why, friends, you are going to do something, but don't know
    what it is.
  In what way has Caesar deserved to be loved by you?
230 Alas, you don't know; I must tell you then.
  You have forgotten the will I told you about.

ALL
  Most true, the will. Let's stay and hear the will.

ANTONY
  Here is the will, with Caesar's seal on it.
  To every Roman citizen he gives—
235 to every single person—one hundred dollars in cash.

SECOND CITIZEN
  Most noble Caesar, we'll revenge his death.

THIRD CITIZEN
  O generous Caesar!

ANTONY
  Hear me with patience.

ALL
  Quiet there!

ANTONY
240 In addition, he has left you all his paths for walking,
  his own landscaped grounds, and newly planted gardens
  on this side of the river Tiber. He has left them to you
  and to your heirs forever as public parks
  to walk in and enjoy yourselves.
  What a Caesar he was! When will there ever be another
245 man like him?

---

to Shakespeare's audience. $100 as the equivalent of 75 drachmas is just a
guess.

FIRST PLEBEIAN
   Never, never. Come, away, away!
   We'll burn his body in the holy place,
   And with the brands fire the traitors' houses.
   Take up the body.

SECOND PLEBEIAN
250   Go fetch fire.

THIRD PLEBEIAN
   Pluck down benches.

FOURTH PLEBEIAN
   Pluck down forms, windows, anything.
      Exit Plebeians [*with Caesar's body*].

ANTONY
   Now let it work. Mischief, thou art afoot,
   Take thou what course thou wilt.
      Enter Servant.
                           How now, fellow?

SERVANT
255   Sir, Octavius is already come to Rome.

ANTONY
   Where is he?

SERVANT
   He and Lepidus* are at Caesar's house.

ANTONY
   And thither will I straight to visit him.
   He comes upon a wish. Fortune is merry,
260   And in this mood will give us anything.

SERVANT
   I heard him say Brutus and Cassius
   Are rid like madmen through the gates of Rome.

ANTONY
   Belike they had some notice of the people
   How I had moved them. Bring me to Octavius.
      Exeunt.

---

257 *Lepidus*   Marcus Aemilius Lepidus, a supporter of Caesar and consul
with him in 46 B.C., was outside Rome with an army at the time of Caesar's

FIRST CITIZEN
Never, never. Come, away, away!
We'll burn his body in the temple,
and with the torches set fire to the traitors' houses.
Take up the body.

SECOND CITIZEN
50   Go get fire.

THIRD CITIZEN
Pull down benches.

FOURTH CITIZEN
Pull down benches, window shutters, anything.
    Exit the Citizens with Caesar's body.

ANTONY
Now let my speech do its work. Spiteful destructiveness
    has been unloosed;
let it take whatever course it pleases.
    Enter Servant.
What do you want, fellow?

SERVANT
55   Sir, Octavius has already come to Rome.

ANTONY
Where is he?

SERVANT
He and Lepidus are at Julius Caesar's house.

ANTONY
And I will go there immediately to visit Octavius.
He comes according to my wish. Luck is with us,
60   and in this merry mood will give us anything.

SERVANT
I heard him say that Brutus and Cassius
have ridden like madmen through the gates of Rome.

ANTONY
They probably had some news about how I moved the people
with my oration. Bring me to Octavius.
    They exit.

---

assassination. He later became one of the Triumvirate with Antony and
Octavius.

[*Scene iii: Rome, a street.*] *Enter* CINNA *the Poet, and after him th*
Plebeians.

CINNA
　　I dreamt tonight that I did feast with Caesar,
　　And things unluckily charge my fantasy.
　　I have no will to wander forth of doors,
　　Yet something leads me forth.
FIRST PLEBEIAN
5　　What is your name?
SECOND PLEBEIAN
　　Whither are you going?
THIRD PLEBEIAN
　　Where do you dwell?
FOURTH PLEBEIAN
　　Are you a married man or a bachelor?
SECOND PLEBEIAN
　　Answer every man directly.
FIRST PLEBEIAN
10　　Ay, and briefly.
FOURTH PLEBEIAN
　　Ay, and wisely.
THIRD PLEBEIAN
　　Ay, and truly, you were best.
CINNA
　　What is my name? Whither am I going? Where do I dwell? Am
　　a married man or a bachelor? Then, to answer every man directl
15　　and briefly, wisely and truly: wisely I say, I am a bachelor.
SECOND PLEBEIAN
　　That's as much as to say, they are fools that marry. You'll bea
　　me a bang for that, I fear. Proceed directly.
CINNA
　　Directly I am going to Caesar's funeral.
FIRST PLEBEIAN
　　As a friend or an enemy?
CINNA
20　　As a friend.
SECOND PLEBEIAN
　　The matter is answered directly.

Scene iii: A street in Rome. Enter CINNA *the Poet, and after him a mob of citizens coming from Antony's oration.*

CINNA
>I dreamt last night that I was feasting with Caesar,
>and my imagination is burdened with thoughts of evil omen.
>I don't have any desire to wander about in the street,
>yet something moves me to go out.

FIRST CITIZEN
5
>What is your name?

SECOND CITIZEN
>Where are you going?

THIRD CITIZEN
>Where do you live?

FOURTH CITIZEN
>Are you a married man or a bachelor?

SECOND CITIZEN
>Answer everyone without beating around the bush.

FIRST CITIZEN
10
>Yes, and briefly.

FOURTH CITIZEN
>Yes, and wisely.

THIRD CITIZEN
>Yes, and truthfully, you had better.

CINNA
>What is my name? Where am I going? Where do I live?
>>Am I
>a married man or a bachelor? Then, to answer everyone
>>straightforwardly
15
>and briefly, wisely and truthfully: wisely I say, I am a bachelor.

SECOND CITIZEN
>That's as much as to say, they are fools that marry. You'll get
>a punch from me for that kind of answer, I'm afraid.
>>Get right to the point.

CINNA
>I am going straight to Caesar's funeral.

FIRST CITIZEN
>As a friend or an enemy?

CINNA
20
>As a friend.

SECOND CITIZEN
>That question is answered to the point.

FOURTH PLEBEIAN
    For your dwelling—briefly.
CINNA
    Briefly, I dwell by the Capitol.
THIRD PLEBEIAN
    Your name, sir, truly.
CINNA
25   Truly, my name is Cinna.
FIRST PLEBEIAN
    Tear him to pieces, he's a conspirator.
CINNA
    I am Cinna the poet, I am Cinna the poet.
FOURTH PLEBEIAN
    Tear him for his bad verses, tear him for his bad verses.
CINNA
    I am not Cinna the conspirator.
FOURTH PLEBEIAN
30   It is no matter, his name's Cinna; pluck but his name out of his
    heart, and turn him going.
THIRD PLEBEIAN
    Tear him, tear him! Come, brands, ho! firebrands! To Brutus', to
    Cassius', burn all! Some to Decius' house and some to Casca's;
    some to Ligarius'. Away, go!
        Exeunt all the Plebeians [with CINNA].

Act IV, [*Scene i: Rome, Antony's house*]. *Enter* ANTONY, OCTAVIUS,
and LEPIDUS.

ANTONY
    These many then shall die; their names are pricked.
OCTAVIUS
    Your brother too must die. Consent you, Lepidus?
LEPIDUS
    I do consent—
OCTAVIUS
                Prick him down, Antony.
LEPIDUS
    Upon condition Publius shall not live,
5   Who is your sister's son, Mark Antony.

FOURTH CITIZEN
Where's your home—briefly.
CINNA
Briefly, I live by the Capitol.
THIRD CITIZEN
Your name, sir, truthfully.
CINNA
25   Truthfully, my name is Cinna.
FIRST CITIZEN
Tear him to pieces, he's a conspirator.
CINNA
I am Cinna the poet, I am Cinna the poet.
FOURTH CITIZEN
Kill him for his bad verses, kill him for his bad verses.
CINNA
I am not Cinna the conspirator.
FOURTH CITIZEN
30   It doesn't matter, his name's Cinna. Just extract his name
and set him on his way.
THIRD CITIZEN
Kill him, kill him! Come, torches, right here! firebrands!
   To Brutus's house, to
Cassius's, burn everything! Some go to Decius's house and
   some to Casca's;
some to Ligarius's. Away, let's go!
   Exit all the citizens with CINNA.

Act IV, Scene i: Rome, at Antony's house. Enter ANTONY, OC-
TAVIUS, *and* LEPIDUS.

ANTONY
All these men shall die; their names are checked off.
OCTAVIUS
Your brother too must die. Do you agree, Lepidus?
LEPIDUS
I consent—
OCTAVIUS
Check him off, Antony.
LEPIDUS
Provided that Publius shall not live,
5   who is your sister's son, Mark Antony.

ANTONY

He shall not live. Look, with a spot I damn him.
But, Lepidus, go you to Caesar's house.
Fetch the will hither, and we shall determine
How to cut off some charge in legacies.

LEPIDUS

10   What, shall I find you here?

OCTAVIUS

Or here, or at the Capitol.
Exit LEPIDUS.

ANTONY

This is a slight unmeritable man,
Meet to be sent on errands. Is it fit,
The threefold world* divided, he should stand
One of the three to share it?

OCTAVIUS

15   So you thought him,
And took his voice who should be pricked to die
In our black sentence and proscription.

ANTONY

Octavius, I have seen more days than you;
And though we lay these honors on this man
20   To ease ourselves of divers sland'rous loads,
He shall but bear them as the ass bears gold,
To groan and sweat under the business,
Either led or driven as we point the way;
And having brought our treasure where we will,
25   Then take we down his load, and turn him off,
Like to the empty ass, to shake his ears
And graze in commons.

OCTAVIUS

                              You may do your will;
But he's a tried and valiant soldier.

ANTONY

So is my horse, Octavius, and for that
30   I do appoint him store of provender.

---

14 *threefold world* when the Triumvirate was established in 43 B.C., Antony, Octavius, and Lepidus each laid claim to a different sphere of influence in the Roman Empire (extending over Europe, Africa, and Asia).

ANTONY

He shall not live. Look, with a mark next to his name
   I damn him.
But, Lepidus, go to Caesar's house.
Bring the will here, and we shall figure out
how to cut off some of the expenses in Caesar's legacies.

LEPIDUS

10 Then shall I find you here?

OCTAVIUS

Either here or at the Capitol.
   Exit LEPIDUS.

ANTONY

He is a foolish, insignificant man,
suitable to be sent on errands. Is it right,
with the threefold world divided among us, that he should be
one of the three to share it?

OCTAVIUS

15 You thought him worthy enough
and consulted his opinion about who should be checked off
in our death sentences and banishments.

ANTONY

Octavius, I am older than you are,
and though we load this man with honors,
20 in order to lighten our own burden of slander,
he shall only bear them as the ass carries gold,
to groan and sweat under its heavy load,
either led or driven as we show the way.
And having brought our treasure where we want him to,
25 then we remove his burden and get rid of him,
like an unloaded ass, who will have plenty of time to shake
   his ears
and be put to pasture at public expense.

OCTAVIUS

You may do what you want,
but Lepidus is an experienced and brave soldier.

ANTONY

So is my horse, Octavius, and because of that
30 I provide him with an ample supply of fodder.

It is a creature that I teach to fight,
To wind, to stop, to run directly on,
His corporal motion governed by my spirit.
And, in some taste, is Lepidus but so.
35   He must be taught, and trained, and bid go forth:
A barren-spirited fellow; one that feeds
On objects, arts, and imitations,
Which, out of use and staled by other men,
Begin his fashion. Do not talk of him
40   But as a property. And now, Octavius,
Listen great things. Brutus and Cassius
Are levying powers. We must straight make head.
Therefore let our alliance be combined,
Our best friends made, our means stretched;
45   And let us presently go sit in council
How covert matters may be best disclosed,
And open perils surest answerèd.

OCTAVIUS
Let us do so; for we are at the stake,*
And bayed about with many enemies;
50   And some that smile have in their hearts, I fear,
Millions of mischiefs.
          Exeunt.

[*Scene ii: The camp near Sardis*; before the tent of Brutus.*] *Drum*
Enter BRUTUS, LUCILIUS, [LUCIUS,] *and the Army.* TITINIUS *an*
PINDARUS *meet them.*

BRUTUS
Stand, ho!

LUCILIUS
Give the word, ho! and stand!

BRUTUS
What now, Lucilius, is Cassius near?

LUCILIUS
He is at hand, and Pindarus is come
5   To do you salutation from his master.

---

48 *at the stake*   an image from the Elizabethan sport of bearbaiting, i
which a bear was chained to a stake in the middle of an arena and the
attacked by dogs.

My horse is a creature that I teach to fight,
to turn about, to stop, to run straight on,
his bodily motion controlled by my spirit.
And, in some measure, Lepidus is much the same.
35 He must be taught, and trained, and ordered to do things.
He's a dull, unimaginative fellow, someone who thrives
on "the sights," knick-knacks, and fads,
which, when they are no longer popular (and made stale
by other men),
then Lepidus takes them over to begin his own fashion.
Don't take him more seriously
40 than a mere prop. And now, Octavius,
listen to something important. Brutus and Cassius
are raising an army; we must immediately do likewise.
Therefore let us strengthen our alliances,
rally our best friends to our cause, and stretch our resources
as far as they will go.
45 And let us immediately meet among ourselves to discuss
how pitfalls may be best revealed,
and obvious dangers most successfully opposed.

OCTAVIUS
Let us do so, because, like the bear in a bearbaiting, we are
chained to the stake
and set upon by many enemies.
50 And some of those who smile at us are, I fear, plotting
countless harms against us.
They exit.

*Scene ii: A military camp near Sardis; in front of Brutus's tent.
Drums. Enter* BRUTUS, LUCILIUS, LUCIUS, *and the army.*
TITINIUS *and* PINDARUS *meet them.*

BRUTUS
Stop there!
LUCILIUS
Give the command there and stop!
BRUTUS
Greetings, Lucilius. Is Cassius close by?
LUCILIUS
He is very near here, and Pindarus has come
5 to greet you from his master, Cassius.

IV,ii
  Sardis capital of Lydia, a kingdom in western Asia Minor, now part of
western Turkey.

BRUTUS
> He greets me well. Your master, Pindarus,
> In his own change, or by ill officers,
> Hath given me some worthy cause to wish
> Things done undone; but if he be at hand,
> I shall be satisfied.

PINDARUS
10
>   I do not doubt
> But that my noble master will appear
> Such as he is, full of regard and honor.

BRUTUS
> He is not doubted. A word, Lucilius,
> How he received you. Let me be resolved.

LUCILIUS
15
> With courtesy and with respect enough,
> But not with such familiar instances,
> Nor with such free and friendly conference
> As he hath used of old.

BRUTUS
>   Thou hast described
> A hot friend cooling. Ever note, Lucilius,
20
> When love begins to sicken and decay
> It useth an enforcèd ceremony.
> There are no tricks in plain and simple faith;
> But hollow men, like horses hot at hand,
> Make gallant show and promise of their mettle;
>   *Low march within.*
25
> But when they should endure the bloody spur,
> They fall their crests, and like deceitful jades
> Sink in the trial. Comes his army on?

LUCILIUS
> They mean this night in Sardis to be quartered.
> The greater part, the horse in general,
> Are come with Cassius.
>   *Enter* CASSIUS *and his Powers.*

BRUTUS
30
>   Hark, he is arrived.
> March gently on to meet him.

BRUTUS
  He sends his greetings by a worthy messenger.
    Your master, Pindarus,
  either because of his own changed feelings toward me, or
      through the influence of bad officers,
  has given me strong reason to wish that
  things done could be undone. But if he is nearby,
  I expect to receive a full explanation from him.
PINDARUS
10 I do not doubt
  that my noble master will appear
  exactly as he really is: full of respect for you and concern for
      his own honor.
BRUTUS
  I don't suspect him. (*To Lucilius*) A word with you, Lucilius.
  Tell me how Cassius received you. Let me be fully informed.
LUCILIUS
15 With enough courtesy and respect,
  but not with such congenial signs,
  nor with such free and friendly conversation
  as he used to show.
BRUTUS
  You have described
  a warm friend cooling. Always note, Lucilius,
20 that when love begins to weaken and diminish,
  it insists on a forced politeness.
  There are no false displays in genuine and simple fidelity;
  but insincere men, like horses raring to go,
  make a big show and promise of their eager courage,
      Muffled sound of drums, playing a march off-stage.
  but when it comes time to respond to their rider's
25   bloody spurring,
  they slack off, and like deceitful nags,
  they fail when put to the test. Is Cassius's army coming?
LUCILIUS
  They intend to stay in Sardis tonight.
  The larger part—all the cavalry—
  have come with Cassius.
      Enter CASSIUS *and his army.*
BRUTUS
30 Look, he has arrived.
  March slowly on to meet him.

CASSIUS
  Stand, ho!

BRUTUS
  Stand, ho! Speak the word along.

[FIRST SOLDIER]
  Stand!

[SECOND SOLDIER]
35 Stand!

[THIRD SOLDIER]
  Stand!

CASSIUS
  Most noble brother,* you have done me wrong.

BRUTUS
  Judge me, you gods; wrong I mine enemies?
  And if not so, how should I wrong a brother?

CASSIUS
40 Brutus, this sober form of yours hides wrongs,
  And when you do them—

BRUTUS
                         Cassius, be content.
  Speak your griefs softly; I do know you well.
  Before the eyes of both our armies here,
  Which should perceive nothing but love from us,
45 Let us not wrangle. Bid them move away;
  Then in my tent, Cassius, enlarge your griefs,
  And I will give you audience.

CASSIUS
                         Pindarus,
  Bid our commanders lead their charges off
  A little from this ground.

BRUTUS
50 Lucius, do you the like; and let no man
  Come to our tent till we have done our conference.
  Let Lucilius and Titinius guard our door.
      Exeunt.

---

37 *brother* literally, brother-in-law (see note at 2.1.70), although Cassius
may also mean it in the wider sense of "dear friend."

CASSIUS
Stop there!

BRUTUS
Stop there! Give the command to the armies.

FIRST SOLDIER
Stop!

SECOND SOLDIER
35   Stop!

THIRD SOLDIER
Stop!

CASSIUS
Most noble brother, you have done me wrong.

BRUTUS
Judge me, you gods. Do I wrong my enemies?
And if I don't do that, why should I wrong a brother?

CASSIUS
Brutus, this restrained, formal manner of yours hides the
40   wrongs you have done me,
and when you commit them—

BRUTUS
Cassius, keep calm.
Speak your complaints quietly; after all, I know you well.
Before the eyes of both our armies here,
which should see nothing but mutual love from us,
45   let us not quarrel. Order the armies to move away,
then in my tent, Cassius, express your complaints freely,
and I will listen to you.

CASSIUS
Pindarus,
order our commanders to lead their troops
a little way off from this place.

BRUTUS
50   Lucius, do likewise, and don't let anyone
come to our tent until we have finished our conference.
Let Lucilius and Titinius guard our door.
> *All exit except* BRUTUS *and* CASSIUS, *who go into
> Brutus's tent.*

[Scene iii: The camp near Sardis; within the tent of Brutus.] BRUTU
and CASSIUS *remain.*

CASSIUS
    That you have wronged me doth appear in this:
    You have condemned and noted Lucius Pella
    For taking bribes here of the Sardians;
    Wherein my letters, praying on his side,
5   Because I knew the man, was slighted off.

BRUTUS
    You wronged yourself to write in such a case.

CASSIUS
    In such a time as this it is not meet
    That every nice offense should bear his comment.

BRUTUS
    Let me tell you, Cassius, you yourself
10 Are much condemned to have an itching palm,
    To sell and mart your offices for gold
    To undeservers.

CASSIUS
                    I, an itching palm?
    You know that you are Brutus that speaks this,
    Or, by the gods, this speech were else your last.

BRUTUS
15 The name of Cassius honors this corruption,
    And chastisement doth therefore hide his head.

CASSIUS
    Chastisement?

BRUTUS
    Remember March, the ides of March remember.
    Did not great Julius bleed for justice sake?
20 What villain touched his body that did stab,
    And not for justice? What, shall one of us,
    That struck the foremost man of all this world
    But for supporting robbers, shall we now
    Contaminate our fingers with base bribes,
25 And sell the mighty space of our large honors
    For so much trash as may be graspèd thus?

Scene iii: The military camp near Sardis; within Brutus's tent.

CASSIUS
> The wrong you have done me is apparent in this:
> you condemned and publicly disgraced Lucius Pella
> for taking bribes here from the Sardians,
> but my letter, asking you to let him off
> 5 because I knew him, was contemptuously disregarded.

BRUTUS
> You did wrong to yourself to ask for mercy in such an
>   obviously guilty case.

CASSIUS
> In times like these it is not proper
> that every trivial offense should be punished.

BRUTUS
> Let me tell you something, Cassius. You yourself
> 10 are much accused of having a palm that itches for bribes,
> and that you use your good name to sell public offices for cash
> to undeserving men.

CASSIUS (*trying to control his rage*)
> I, an itching palm?
> If it weren't for the fact that Brutus speaks these insults,
> I swear, by the gods, this speech would be your last.

BRUTUS
> 15 The good name of Cassius protects this corruption,
> and therefore you escape punishment.

CASSIUS
> Punishment?

BRUTUS
> Remember March, remember the ides of March.
> Did not great Julius bleed for the sake of justice?
> 20 What villain touched his body to stab him,
> who didn't do it for justice? What, shall one of us,
> who struck down the foremost man of all this world
> only because he supported crooks, shall we now
> dirty our hands with petty bribes,
> 25 and use our integrity as a front for influence-peddling
> to get as much worthless money as we can grasp thus (*with a
>   gesture of contempt*)?

I had rather be a dog, and bay the moon,
Than such a Roman.

CASSIUS

Brutus, bait not me,
I'll not endure it. You forget yourself
To hedge me in. I am a soldier, I,
Older in practice, abler than yourself
To make conditions.

BRUTUS

Go to; you are not, Cassius.

CASSIUS
I am.

BRUTUS
I say you are not.

CASSIUS
Urge me no more, I shall forget myself.
Have mind upon your health. Tempt me no farther.

BRUTUS
Away, slight man!

CASSIUS
Is't possible?

BRUTUS
Hear me, for I will speak.
Must I give way and room to your rash choler?
Shall I be frighted when a madman stares?

CASSIUS
O ye gods, ye gods! Must I endure all this?

BRUTUS
All this? Ay, more. Fret till your proud heart break.
Go show your slaves how choleric you are,
And make your bondmen tremble. Must I budge?
Must I observe you? Must I stand and crouch
Under your testy humor? By the gods,
You shall digest the venom of your spleen
Though it do split you. For, from this day forth,
I'll use you for my mirth, yea, for my laughter,
When you are waspish.

CASSIUS
Is it come to this?

I had rather be a dog and howl at the moon
than that kind of Roman.

CASSIUS

Brutus, don't taunt me—
I won't permit it. You forget your own dignity
to close in on me like this. I myself am a soldier,
more experienced in practical matters, better able than you
to manage things.

BRUTUS

Come off it; you are not, Cassius.

CASSIUS

I am.

BRUTUS

I say you are not.

CASSIUS

Don't push me any further or I may forget myself.
Look out for your own safety. Provoke me no further.

BRUTUS

Buzz off, weakling!

CASSIUS

Is it possible?

BRUTUS

Now hear me, because I want to speak.
Must I put up with and make allowances for your bad temper?
Shall I be frightened when a madman glares at me?

CASSIUS

O you gods, you gods! Do I have to stand for all this?

BRUTUS

All this? Yes, and more. Eat your heart out.
Go show your slaves how angry you are
and make your serfs tremble. Must I flinch?
Must I be humble to you? Must I stand and bow
because of your peevish disposition? By the gods,
you will swallow your own anger in silence
even though you burst. Because, from this day on,
I'll treat you like a joke—yes, I'll laugh at you
when you're as angry as a wasp.

CASSIUS

Is this the way it's all turned out?

BRUTUS

You say you are a better soldier.
Let it appear so; make your vaunting true,
And it shall please me well. For mine own part,
I shall be glad to learn of noble men.

CASSIUS

55 You wrong me every way; you wrong me, Brutus.
I said an elder soldier, not a better.
Did I say "better"?

BRUTUS

If you did, I care not.

CASSIUS

When Caesar lived, he durst not thus have moved me.

BRUTUS

Peace, peace! You durst not so have tempted him.

CASSIUS

60 I durst not?

BRUTUS

No.

CASSIUS

What, durst not tempt him?

BRUTUS

For your life you durst not.

CASSIUS

Do not presume too much upon my love;
I may do that I shall be sorry for.

BRUTUS

65 You have done that you should be sorry for.
There is no terror, Cassius, in your threats;
For I am armed so strong in honesty
That they pass by me as the idle wind,
Which I respect not. I did send to you
70 For certain sums of gold, which you denied me;
For I can raise no money by vile means.
By heaven, I had rather coin my heart,
And drop my blood for drachmas* than to wring
From the hard hands of peasants their vile trash
75 By any indirection. I did send
To you for gold to pay my legions,

---

73 *drachmas*   see note at 3.2.235.

BRUTUS

You say you are a better soldier.
Why don't you prove it? Make your boasts come true,
and it shall please me well. For my part,
I would be glad to learn something from noble men.

CASSIUS

55 You do me wrong in every way; you really wrong me, Brutus.
I said a more experienced soldier, not a better.
Did I say "better"?

BRUTUS

If you did, I don't care.

CASSIUS

When Caesar was alive, he wouldn't dare to exasperate me
like this.

BRUTUS

Be quiet, be quiet! You wouldn't dare to tempt him as
you have me.

CASSIUS

60 I wouldn't dare?

BRUTUS

No.

CASSIUS

What, I wouldn't dare to tempt him?

BRUTUS

You wouldn't dare, for fear of losing your life.

CASSIUS

Do not take my love too much for granted;
I may do something that I shall be sorry for.

BRUTUS

65 You have already done something you should be sorry for.
There is no terror, Cassius, in your threats,
because my own integrity is an armor so strong
that they blow by me like the idle wind,
which I pay no attention to. I asked you
70 for certain sums of money, which you denied me,
for I am incapable of raising money by underhanded means.
By heaven, I had rather turn my own heart into coins
and shed my blood for dollars than try to wring
any vile, trashy money out of the
75 hard hands of peasants by crooked means. I sent
to you for gold to pay my troops,

Which you denied me. Was that done like Cassius?
Should I have answered Caius Cassius so?
When Marcus Brutus grows so covetous
80   To lock such rascal counters from his friends,
Be ready, gods, with all your thunderbolts;
Dash him to pieces.

CASSIUS
                    I denied you not.

BRUTUS
    You did.

CASSIUS
                    I did not. He was but a fool
That brought my answer back. Brutus hath rived my heart.
85   A friend should bear his friend's infirmities,
But Brutus makes mine greater than they are.

BRUTUS
    I do not, till you practice them on me.

CASSIUS
    You love me not.

BRUTUS
                    I do not like your faults.

CASSIUS
    A friendly eye could never see such faults.

BRUTUS
90   A flatterer's would not, though they do appear
As huge as high Olympus.*

CASSIUS
    Come, Antony, and young Octavius, come;
Revenge yourselves alone on Cassius,
For Cassius is aweary of the world:
95   Hated by one he loves, braved by his brother,
Checked like a bondman, all his faults observed,
Set in a notebook, learned, and conned by rote
To cast into my teeth. O I could weep
My spirit from mine eyes! There is my dagger,
100   And here my naked breast; within, a heart
Dearer than Pluto's mine,* richer than gold.
If that thou be'st a Roman, take it forth.
I, that denied thee gold, will give my heart.

---

91 *Olympus*   see note at 3.1.74.
101 *Pluto's mine*   Pluto, god of the underworld, ruled over all the riches

which you denied me. Was that done like Cassius?
Would I have answered you this way?
When Marcus Brutus grows so miserly
80 as to lock up such worthless coins from his friends,
be ready, gods, with all your thunderbolts:
shatter him to pieces.

CASSIUS
I didn't deny you.

BRUTUS
You did.

CASSIUS
I did not. He was clearly a fool
who brought back my answer. Brutus has broken my heart.
85 A friend should tolerate his friend's weaknesses,
but Brutus makes mine greater than they are.

BRUTUS
I do not, until you try to trick me with them.

CASSIUS
You don't love me.

BRUTUS
I do not like your faults.

CASSIUS
A friendly eye could never see such faults.

BRUTUS
90 The eye of a flatterer would not, even if they appear
as huge as the high mountain of Olympus.

CASSIUS
Come, Antony, and young Octavius, come.
Revenge yourselves on Cassius alone,
because Cassius is weary of living:
95 hated by someone he loves, defied by his brother,
rebuked like a slave, all his faults pointed out,
set in a notebook, learned, and memorized
to throw up in my face. O I could weep
my manly spirit out from my eyes! There is my dagger,
100 and here is my naked breast; within is a heart
of greater value than all the mines of Pluto, richer than gold.
If you really are a Roman, take my heart.
I, that denied you gold, will give you my heart.

---

in mines, although there was a common confusion between Pluto and Plutus,
the god of wealth.

Strike as thou didst at Caesar; for I know,
When thou didst hate him worst, thou lovedst him better
Than ever thou lovedst Cassius.

BRUTUS
Sheathe your dagger.
Be angry when you will, it shall have scope.
Do what you will, dishonor shall be humor.
O Cassius, you are yokèd with a lamb,
That carries anger as the flint bears fire;
Who, much enforcèd, shows a hasty spark,
And straight is cold again.

CASSIUS
Hath Cassius lived
To be but mirth and laughter to his Brutus,
When grief and blood ill-tempered* vexeth him?

BRUTUS
When I spoke that, I was ill-tempered too.

CASSIUS
Do you confess so much? Give me your hand.

BRUTUS
And my heart too.

CASSIUS
O Brutus!

BRUTUS
What's the matter?

CASSIUS
Have not you love enough to bear with me,
When that rash humor which my mother gave me
Makes me forgetful?

BRUTUS
Yes, Cassius, and from henceforth,
When you are over-earnest with your Brutus,
He'll think your mother chides, and leave you so.
Enter a Poet, [*followed by* LUCILIUS, TITINIUS, *and* LUCIUS].

---

114 *blood ill-tempered* a disposition in which the four humors of the
body (blood, phlegm, choler, and black bile) are not properly "tempered," or
in equilibrium.

Strike as you did at Caesar, because I know,
when you hated him worst, you loved him better
than you ever loved Cassius.

BRUTUS
Put your dagger back in its sheath.
Be angry whenever you want to, you shall have permission to
indulge yourself.
Do what you will. What others think an insult, I shall consider
a mere display of temper.
O Cassius, you are partners with a lamb,
who feels anger as the flintstone feels fire,
which, when struck hard, shows a hasty spark
and is immediately cold again.

CASSIUS
Has Cassius lived until now
only to be a cause of mirth and laughter to his Brutus,
when my grief and badly balanced temperament disturb me?

BRUTUS
When I spoke those angry words, I was out of sorts too.

CASSIUS
Do you confess that? Give me your hand.

BRUTUS
And my heart too.

CASSIUS
O Brutus!

BRUTUS
What's the matter?

CASSIUS
Don't you have enough love to bear with me
when that angry temperament I inherited from my mother
makes me forget myself?

BRUTUS
Yes, Cassius, and from now on
when you take your Brutus too seriously,
he'll think it's your mother who rebukes him, and leave it at that.
    Enter a Poet, followed by LUCILIUS, TITINIUS,
    and LUCIUS.

POET

    Let me go in to see the generals.

    There is some grudge between 'em; 'tis not meet

    They be alone.

LUCILIUS

125   You shall not come to them.

POET

    Nothing but death shall stay me.

CASSIUS

    How now? What's the matter?

POET

    For shame, you generals! What do you mean?

    Love, and be friends, as two such men should be;

130   For I have seen more years, I'm sure, than ye.

CASSIUS

    Ha, ha! How vilely doth this cynic* rhyme!

BRUTUS

    Get you hence, sirrah; saucy fellow, hence!

CASSIUS

    Bear with him, Brutus, 'tis his fashion.

BRUTUS

    I'll know his humor when he knows his time.

135   What should the wars do with these jigging fools?

    Companion, hence!

CASSIUS

                Away, away, be gone!

     Exit Poet.

BRUTUS

    Lucilius and Titinius, bid the commanders

    Prepare to lodge their companies tonight.

CASSIUS

    And come yourselves, and bring Messala with you

    Immediately to us.

     [*Exeunt* LUCILIUS *and* TITINIUS.]

BRUTUS

140   Lucius, a bowl of wine.

     [*Exit* LUCIUS.]

CASSIUS

    I did not think you could have been so angry.

---

131 *cynic*   a Cynic philosopher; also a rude, boorish fellow (from the
Greek word for dog).

POET

Let me go in to see the generals.
There is some grudge between them. It's not right that
they be left alone.

LUCILIUS

125   You shall not go in to see them.

POET

Nothing but death will prevent me.

CASSIUS

What's happening? What's the matter?

POET

For shame, you generals! What do you mean by this quarrel?
Love and be friends, as two such men should be,
130   because I am much older, I'm sure, than you are.

CASSIUS

Ha, ha! How badly does this cynic philosopher rhyme!

BRUTUS

Get going, mister. Wise guy, take off!

CASSIUS

You should tolerate him, Brutus; it's just his way.

BRUTUS

I'll put up with his quirks, when he learns the proper time
    and place for them.
135   What business does war have with these rhymesters?
Friend, be off!

CASSIUS

Away, away, be gone!
    Exit Poet.

BRUTUS

Lucilius and Titinius, order the commanders
to prepare lodging for their companies tonight.

CASSIUS

Then come back yourselves and bring Messala with you
immediately to us.
    Exit LUCILIUS *and* TITINIUS.

BRUTUS

140   Lucius, bring a bowl of wine.
    Exit LUCIUS.

CASSIUS

I did not think you could have been so angry.

BRUTUS
     O Cassius, I am sick of many griefs.

CASSIUS
     Of your philosophy* you make no use,
     If you give place to accidental evils.

BRUTUS
145   No man bears sorrow better. Portia is dead.

CASSIUS
     Ha! Portia?

BRUTUS
     She is dead.

CASSIUS
     How scaped I killing when I crossed you so?
     O insupportable and touching loss!
     Upon what sickness?

BRUTUS
150   Impatient of my absence,
     And grief that young Octavius with Mark Antony
     Have made themselves so strong; for with her death
     That tidings came. With this she fell distract,
     And, her attendants absent, swallowed fire.

CASSIUS
     And died so?

BRUTUS
                         Even so.

CASSIUS
155   O ye immortal gods!
          Enter Boy [LUCIUS] *with wine and tapers.*

BRUTUS
     Speak no more of her. Give me a bowl of wine.
     In this I bury all unkindness, Cassius.
          Drinks.

CASSIUS
     My heart is thirsty for that noble pledge.
     Fill, Lucius, till the wine o'erswell the cup.
160   I cannot drink too much of Brutus' love.
          [*Exit* LUCIUS.]
          Enter TITINIUS *and* MESSALA.

---

143 *philosophy* i.e., Stoicism. As a Stoic, Brutus should be superior to changes in fortune, since the Stoics believed that no evil should affect a man's inner tranquillity and peace of mind.

BRUTUS

O Cassius, I am heavy-hearted with many sorrows.

CASSIUS

You aren't being much of a Stoic
if you let yourself be unsettled by chance misfortunes.

BRUTUS

145 No man endures sorrow better. Portia is dead.

CASSIUS

What! Portia?

BRUTUS

She is dead.

CASSIUS

How did I escape being killed when I contradicted you so much?
O unbearable and tragic loss!
What sickness did she die of?

BRUTUS

150 Unable to bear my absence,
and anxiety because young Octavius with Mark Antony
have made themselves so strong, for that news
came at the same time as the report of her death. At this bad
turn in our fortunes, she became deranged,
and, when her servants were absent, she swallowed hot coals.

CASSIUS

And that's the way she died?

BRUTUS

Just like that.

CASSIUS

155 O you immortal gods!
Enter the boy LUCIUS *with wine and candles.*

BRUTUS

Speak no more of Portia. Give me a bowl of wine.
In this drink I bury all the unkindness of our quarrel, Cassius.
Drinks.

CASSIUS

My heart is thirsty for that noble toast.
Fill, Lucius, until the wine overflows the cup.
160 I cannot drink too much of Brutus's love.
Exit LUCIUS.
Enter TITINIUS *and* MESSALA.

BRUTUS
Come in, Titinius. Welcome, good Messala.
Now sit we close about this taper here,
And call in question our necessities.

CASSIUS
Portia, art thou gone?

BRUTUS
No more, I pray you.

165   Messala, I have here receivèd letters
That young Octavius and Mark Antony
Come down upon us with a mighty power,
Bending their expedition toward Philippi.*

MESSALA
Myself have letters of the selfsame tenure.

BRUTUS
170   With what addition?

MESSALA
That by proscription and bills of outlawry,
Octavius, Antony, and Lepidus
Have put to death an hundred senators.

BRUTUS
Therein our letters do not well agree.

175   Mine speak of seventy senators that died
By their proscriptions, Cicero being one.

CASSIUS
Cicero one?

MESSALA
Cicero is dead,
And by that order of proscription.
Had you your letters from your wife, my lord?*

BRUTUS
180   No, Messala.

MESSALA
Nor nothing in your letters writ of her?

BRUTUS
Nothing, Messala.

MESSALA
That methinks is strange.

BRUTUS
Why ask you? Hear you aught of her in yours?

---

168 *Philippi* a city in Macedonia (now northeastern Greece, near th
Aegean sea-coast). Philippi was hundreds of miles from Sardis, althoug
Shakespeare seems to suggest that they are not very far apart.

BRUTUS
Come in, Titinius. Welcome, good Messala.
Now let us sit close together around this candle here
and discuss what is necessary for us to do.

CASSIUS
Portia, are you gone?

BRUTUS
No more, I beg you.
65 Messala, I have received a letter
saying that young Octavius and Mark Antony
are bearing down on us with a mighty army,
directing their rapid march toward Philippi.

MESSALA
I have a letter with the same information.

BRUTUS
70 What else does it say?

MESSALA
That by condemnation and various legal decrees,
Octavius, Antony, and Lepidus
have put to death a hundred senators.

BRUTUS
In that matter our letters differ.
75 My letter speaks of seventy senators that died
by legal action, Cicero being one.

CASSIUS
Cicero one of them?

MESSALA
Cicero is dead,
and by that order of condemnation.
Did you get a letter from your wife, my lord?

BRUTUS
80 No, Messala.

MESSALA
Nor anything in the letters you received written about her?

BRUTUS
Nothing, Messala.

MESSALA
I think that strange.

BRUTUS
Why do you ask? Did you hear anything of her in your letters?

179-93 This second revelation of Portia's death conflicts with the earlier
account in this scene. It seems to be the original version that was afterwards
revised. Perhaps it was meant to be deleted but was overlooked.

MESSALA
No, my lord.

BRUTUS
185   Now as you are a Roman, tell me true.

MESSALA
Then like a Roman bear the truth I tell;
For certain she is dead, and by strange manner.

BRUTUS
Why, farewell, Portia. We must die, Messala.
With meditating that she must die once,
190   I have the patience to endure it now.

MESSALA
Even so great men great losses should endure.

CASSIUS
I have as much of this in art as you,
But yet my nature could not bear it so.

BRUTUS
Well, to our work alive. What do you think
195   Of marching to Philippi presently?

CASSIUS
I do not think it good.

BRUTUS
                    Your reason?

CASSIUS
                              This it is:
'Tis better that the enemy seek us;
So shall he waste his means, weary his soldiers,
Doing himself offense, whilst we, lying still,
200   Are full of rest, defense, and nimbleness.

BRUTUS
Good reasons must of force give place to better.
The people 'twixt Philippi and this ground
Do stand but in a forced affection;
For they have grudged us contribution.
205   The enemy, marching along by them,
By them shall make a fuller number up,
Come on refreshed, new added, and encouraged;

MESSALA
No, my lord.

BRUTUS
185 Now as you are a Roman, tell me the truth.

MESSALA
Then, like a Roman (i.e., a Stoic), bear the truth I tell;
because she is certainly dead and in a strange manner.

BRUTUS
Why, farewell, Portia. We all must die, Messala.
Knowing that she had to die sometime
190 gives me the strength to endure it now.

MESSALA
In just this way should great men endure great losses.

CASSIUS
I am as much a believer in Stoic strength of will
as you are, Brutus,
but yet my nature could not bear this as you do.

BRUTUS
Well, let us now take up the work of the living. What do
you think
195 of marching to Philippi right away?

CASSIUS
I do not think it's a good idea.

BRUTUS
Your reason?

CASSIUS
This is it:
it's better that the enemy seeks us.
In that way he will waste his resources, weary his soldiers,
and thus do himself harm, while we, lying still,
200 are full of rest, the ability to defend ourselves, and nimbleness.

BRUTUS
Good reasons must, by necessity, give way to better.
The people between Philippi and this place
support us only because they're forced to—
they have begrudged us any aid.
205 The enemy, marching through their territory,
shall increase their numbers by pressing the natives into service;
then advance against us refreshed, newly reinforced,
and encouraged.

From which advantage shall we cut him off
If at Philippi we do face him there,
These people at our back.

CASSIUS

210   Hear me, good brother.

BRUTUS

Under your pardon. You must note beside
That we have tried the utmost of our friends,
Our legions are brimful, our cause is ripe.
The enemy increaseth every day;

215   We, at the height, are ready to decline.
There is a tide in the affairs of men,
Which, taken at the flood, leads on to fortune;
Omitted, all the voyage of their life
Is bound in shallows and in miseries.

220   On such a full sea are we now afloat,
And we must take the current when it serves,
Or lose our ventures.

CASSIUS

Then, with your will, go on. We'll along
Ourselves and meet them at Philippi.

BRUTUS

225   The deep of night is crept upon our talk,
And nature must obey necessity,
Which we will niggard with a little rest.
There is no more to say?

CASSIUS

                               No more. Good night.
Early tomorrow will we rise, and hence.

BRUTUS

Lucius! (*Enter* LUCIUS.) My gown. [*Exit* LUCIUS.] Farewell,
230   good Messala.
Good night, Titinius. Noble, noble Cassius,
Good night, and good repose.

CASSIUS

                               O my dear brother,
This was an ill beginning of the night.
Never come such division 'tween our souls;

We shall cut the enemy off from this advantage
if we attack at Philippi,
with these people at our back.

CASSIUS

210   Hear me, good brother.

BRUTUS

Excuse me. You must also note
that we have gotten all we can expect from our friends,
our troops are at their full strength, and the time is ripe for us.
The enemy increases every day;
215   we, at our pinnacle, are ready to decline.
There is a tide in human affairs,
which, taken at its highest point, leads on to good fortune;
not taken, all the voyage of their life
is confined by shallow water and other miseries.
220   On such a full sea are we now afloat,
and we must use the tide when it serves our purposes,
or lose all we have risked.

CASSIUS

Then, as you wish it, let's proceed. We will accompany the armies
ourselves and meet the enemy at Philippi.

BRUTUS

225   The middle of the night has crept up on our talk,
and human nature must obey physical need,
which we will briefly satisfy with a little rest.
Is there anything else to discuss?

CASSIUS

No more. Good night.
Early tomorrow we will get up and move out.

BRUTUS

Lucius! (*Enter* LUCIUS.) My dressing gown. (*Exit* LUCIUS.)
230   Farewell, good Messala.
Good night, Titinius. Noble, noble Cassius,
good night and sleep well.

CASSIUS

O my dear brother,
this night began badly.
Let such discord never come between our souls—

Let it not, Brutus.

Enter LUCIUS *with the gown.*

BRUTUS

235   Everything is well.

CASSIUS

Good night, my lord.

BRUTUS

                              Good night, good brother.

TITINIUS, MESSALA

Good night, Lord Brutus.

BRUTUS

                                    Farewell every one.

Exeunt [CASSIUS, TITINIUS, *and* MESSALA].

Give me the gown. Where is thy instrument?*

LUCIUS

Here in the tent.

BRUTUS

                              What, thou speak'st drowsily?

240   Poor knave, I blame thee not; thou art o'erwatched.

Call Claudio and some other of my men;

I'll have them sleep on cushions in my tent.

LUCIUS

Varrus and Claudio!

Enter VARRUS *and* CLAUDIO.

VARRUS

Calls my lord?

BRUTUS

245   I pray you, sirs, lie in my tent and sleep;

It may be I shall raise you by and by

On business to my brother Cassius.

VARRUS

So please you, we will stand and watch your pleasure.

BRUTUS

I will not have it so. Lie down, good sirs.

250   It may be I shall otherwise bethink me.

Look, Lucius, here's the book I sought for so;

I put it in the pocket of my gown.

LUCIUS

I was sure your lordship did not give it me.

---

238 *instrument* probably a lute or some related stringed instrument.

don't let it, Brutus.
> *Enter* LUCIUS *with the dressing gown.*

BRUTUS

235   Everything is well.

CASSIUS

Good night, my lord.

BRUTUS

Good night, good brother.

TITINIUS, MESSALA

Good night, Lord Brutus.

BRUTUS

Farewell every one.
> *Exit* CASSIUS, TITINIUS, *and* MESSALA.

Give me the dressing gown. Where is your instrument?

LUCIUS

Here in the tent.

BRUTUS

What, you sound very drowsy.

240   Poor lad, I don't blame you; you're overtired.

Call Claudio and some other of my men;

I'll have them sleep on cushions in my tent.

LUCIUS

Varrus and Claudio!
> *Enter* VARRUS *and* CLAUDIO.

VARRUS

Does my lord call?

BRUTUS

245   I beg you, sirs, lie in my tent and sleep.

I may wake you up very soon

and send you on an errand to my brother Cassius.

VARRUS

If it pleases you, we will stand and attend to your wishes.

BRUTUS

I don't want you to tire yourselves. Lie down, good sirs.

Maybe I shall change my mind and not have any business

250   for you.

Look, Lucius, here's the book I was searching for;

I put it in the pocket of my dressing gown.

LUCIUS

I was sure that your lordship did not give it to me.

BRUTUS
Bear with me, good boy, I am much forgetful.
255   Canst thou hold up thy heavy eyes awhile,
And touch thy instrument a strain or two?

LUCIUS
Ay, my lord, an't please you.

BRUTUS
                              It does, my boy.
I trouble thee too much, but thou art willing.

LUCIUS
It is my duty, sir.

BRUTUS
260   I should not urge thy duty past thy might;
I know young bloods look for a time of rest.

LUCIUS
I have slept, my lord, already.

BRUTUS
It was well done, and thou shalt sleep again;
I will not hold thee long. If I do live,
265   I will be good to thee.
              Music, and a song.
This is a sleepy tune. O murd'rous slumber!*
Layest thou thy leaden mace upon my boy,
That plays thee music? Gentle knave, good night.
I will not do thee so much wrong to wake thee.
270   If thou dost nod, thou break'st thy instrument;
I'll take it from thee; and, good boy, good night.
Let me see, let me see. Is not the leaf turned down
Where I left reading? Here it is, I think.
              Enter the GHOST OF CAESAR.
How ill this taper burns. Ha! who comes here?
275   I think it is the weakness of mine eyes
That shapes this monstrous apparition.
It comes upon me. Art thou any thing?
Art thou some god, some angel, or some devil,
That mak'st my blood cold and my hair to stare?
280   Speak to me what thou art.

---

266   *murd'rous slumber*   sleep is, conventionally, an image of death.

BRUTUS
Bear with me, good boy, I am very forgetful.
255   Can you keep your heavy eyes open awhile
and play a tune or two on your instrument?

LUCIUS
Yes, my lord, if it pleases you.

BRUTUS
It does, my boy.
I trouble you too much, but you are willing.

LUCIUS
It is my duty, sir.

BRUTUS
260   I shouldn't insist that you do your duty beyond your strength.
I know that young people need a lot of sleep.

LUCIUS
I have slept, my lord, already.

BRUTUS
I am glad you did, and you will sleep again;
I will not keep you long. If I manage to stay alive,
265   I will be good to you.
      Music, and a song.
This tune is like a lullaby. (*Lucius falls asleep.*) O murdering
    slumber!
Do you lay your heavy staff on my boy,
who plays music for you? Gentle lad, good night.
I will not do you so much wrong as to wake you.
If your head falls forward in sleep, you will break
270   your instrument.
I'll take it away from you, and, good boy, good night.
Let me see, let me see. Isn't the page turned down
where I left off reading? Here it is, I think.
    Enter the GHOST OF CAESAR.
How dimly this candle burns. What! Who comes here?
275   I think it must be the weakness of my eyes
that evokes this monstrous ghost.
It comes toward me. Are you any thing?
Are you some god, some angel, or some devil,
that turns my blood cold and makes my hair stand on end?
280   Speak to me and tell me what you are.

GHOST
    Thy evil spirit, Brutus.
BRUTUS
                              Why com'st thou?
GHOST
    To tell thee thou shalt see me at Philippi.
BRUTUS
    Well; then I shall see thee again?
GHOST
    Ay, at Philippi.
BRUTUS
285   Why, I will see thee at Philippi then.
            [*Exit* GHOST.]
        Now I have taken heart thou vanishest.
        Ill spirit, I would hold more talk with thee.
        Boy! Lucius! Varrus! Claudio! Sirs, awake!
        Claudio!
LUCIUS
290   The strings, my lord, are false.
BRUTUS
        He thinks he still is at his instrument.
        Lucius, awake!
LUCIUS
        My lord?
BRUTUS
        Didst thou dream, Lucius, that thou so criedst out?
LUCIUS
295   My lord, I do not know that I did cry.
BRUTUS
        Yes, that thou didst. Didst thou see anything?
LUCIUS
        Nothing, my lord.
BRUTUS
        Sleep again, Lucius. Sirrah Claudio!
        [*To Varrus*] Fellow thou, awake!
VARRUS
300   My lord.
CLAUDIO
        My lord.

GHOST
Your evil spirit, Brutus.

BRUTUS
Why do you come?

GHOST
To tell you that you shall see me at Philippi.

BRUTUS
Well; then I shall see you again?

GHOST
Yes, at Philippi.

BRUTUS
85   Why, I will see you at Philippi then.
       Exit GHOST.
Now that I have gotten my courage back you vanish.
Evil spirit, I would like to talk further with you.
Boy! Lucius! Varrus! Claudio! Sirs, awake!
Claudio!

LUCIUS
90   The strings, my lord, are out of tune.

BRUTUS
He thinks he is still playing his instrument.
Lucius, awake!

LUCIUS
My lord?

BRUTUS
Were you dreaming, Lucius, that you cried out so?

LUCIUS
95   My lord, I was not aware that I cried out.

BRUTUS
Yes, you certainly did. Did you see anything?

LUCIUS
Nothing, my lord.

BRUTUS
Go back to sleep, Lucius. My good man Claudio!
(*To Varrus*) You, fellow, awake!

VARRUS
100   My lord.

CLAUDIO
My lord.

BRUTUS
  Why did you so cry out, sirs, in your sleep?
BOTH
  Did we, my lord?
BRUTUS
                Ay. Saw you anything?
VARRUS
  No, my lord, I saw nothing.
CLAUDIO
                Nor I, my lord.
BRUTUS
305 Go and commend me to my brother Cassius.
  Bid him set on his powers betimes before,
  And we will follow.
BOTH
              It shall be done, my lord.
      Exeunt.

Act V, [Scene i: Near Philippi]. Enter OCTAVIUS, ANTONY, *and their Army.*

OCTAVIUS
  Now, Antony, our hopes are answerèd.
  You said the enemy would not come down,
  But keep the hills and upper regions.
  It proves not so. Their battles are at hand;
5 They mean to warn us at Philippi here,
  Answering before we do demand of them.
ANTONY
  Tut, I am in their bosoms, and I know
  Wherefore they do it. They could be content
  To visit other places, and come down
10 With fearful bravery, thinking by this face
  To fasten in our thoughts that they have courage;
  But 'tis not so.
      Enter a Messenger.
MESSENGER
            Prepare you, generals;
  The enemy comes on in gallant show.

BRUTUS
Why did you cry out so loudly, sirs, in your sleep?
BOTH
Did we, my lord?
BRUTUS
Yes. Did you see anything?
VARRUS
No, my lord, I saw nothing.
CLAUDIO   •
Neither did I, my lord.
BRUTUS
305   Go and pay my respects to my brother Cassius.
Order him to advance with his army early in the morning
     before me,
and my army will follow.
BOTH
It shall be done, my lord.
          They exit.

Act V, Scene i: Near Philippi. Enter OCTAVIUS, ANTONY, *and their army.*

OCTAVIUS
Now, Antony, our hopes are realized.
You said the enemy would not come down,
but would keep to the hills and the higher territory.
It turns out not to be true. Their armies are at hand.
5   They intend to summon us here at Philippi,
appearing to oppose us before we even challenge them to fight.
ANTONY
It doesn't matter, because I have my spies in their camp,
     and I know
why they do it. They would prefer
to be elsewhere, and then come down on us
with a frightening show of defiance, thinking by this
10   grand appearance
to persuade us that they have courage—
but it's not true.
          Enter a Messenger.
MESSENGER
Get ready, generals.
The enemy advances with a splendid display.

Their bloody sign of battle is hung out,
15   And something to be done immediately.
ANTONY
    Octavius, lead your battle softly on
    Upon the left hand of the even field.
OCTAVIUS
    Upon the right hand I; keep thou the left.
ANTONY
    Why do you cross me in this exigent?
OCTAVIUS
20   I do not cross you; but I will do so.
        March.
        Drum. Enter BRUTUS, CASSIUS, *and their Army;* [LUCILIUS,
        TITINIUS, MESSALA, *and others*].
BRUTUS
    They stand, and would have parley.
CASSIUS
    Stand fast, Titinius; we must out and talk.
OCTAVIUS
    Mark Antony, shall we give sign of battle?
ANTONY
    No, Caesar, we will answer on their charge.
25   Make forth; the generals would have some words.
OCTAVIUS
    Stir not until the signal.
BRUTUS
    Words before blows. Is it so, countrymen?
OCTAVIUS
    Not that we love words better, as you do.
BRUTUS
    Good words are better than bad strokes, Octavius.
ANTONY
30   In your bad strokes, Brutus, you give good words;
    Witness the hole you made in Caesar's heart,
    Crying, "Long live! Hail, Caesar!"
CASSIUS
                                Antony,
    The posture of your blows are yet unknown;
    But for your words, they rob the Hybla* bees,
    And leave them honeyless.

---

34 *Hybla*   a mountain in Sicily and a town proverbially famous for its
honey.

Their bloody battle-flag is unfurled,
and the situation calls for immediate action.

ANTONY

Octavius , lead your army slowly forward
on the left side of the level field.

OCTAVIUS

I will take the right side ; you keep to the left.

ANTONY

Why do you contradict me at this critical moment ?

OCTAVIUS

I don't contradict you, but I will do as I please.

> *Sounds of a march. Drums. Enter, at one side of the stage,*
> BRUTUS, CASSIUS, *and their army*; LUCILIUS, TI-
> TINIUS, MESSALA, *and others in the service of* BRUTUS
> *and* CASSIUS.

BRUTUS

They've stopped and would like to confer with us.

CASSIUS

Hold it there, Titinius. We must go out and talk.

OCTAVIUS

Mark Antony, shall we give the sign for immediate battle ?

ANTONY

No, Caesar, we will meet their attack when they make it.
Go forward ; their generals would like to speak with us.

OCTAVIUS (*to his army*)

Do not move until the signal is given.

BRUTUS

Words before blows. Is that the way it is, my countrymen ?

OCTAVIUS

It's not that we love words better than blows, as you do.

BRUTUS

Good words are better than bad blows, Octavius.

ANTONY

With your bad blows, Brutus, you always give good words.
Witness the hole you made in Caesar's heart,
while crying out, "Long live ! Hail, Caesar !"

CASSIUS

Antony,
the kind of blows you are able to strike is still unknown,
but as for your sweet words, they rob the Hybla bees
and leave them without honey.

ANTONY

35   Not stingless too.

BRUTUS

O yes, and soundless too;
For you have stol'n their buzzing, Antony,
And very wisely threat before you sting.

ANTONY

Villains, you did not so when your vile daggers
40   Hacked one another in the sides of Caesar.
You showed your teeth like apes, and fawned like hounds,
And bowed like bondmen, kissing Caesar's feet;
Whilst damnèd Casca, like a cur, behind
Struck Caesar on the neck. O you flatterers!

CASSIUS

45   Flatterers? Now, Brutus, thank yourself;
This tongue had not offended so today
If Cassius might have ruled.

OCTAVIUS

Come, come, the cause. If arguing make us sweat,
The proof of it will turn to redder drops.
50   Look, I draw a sword against conspirators;
When think you that the sword goes up again?
Never till Caesar's three and thirty wounds
Be well avenged, or till another Caesar
Have added slaughter to the sword of traitors.

BRUTUS

55   Caesar, thou canst not die by traitors' hands,
Unless thou bring'st them with thee.

OCTAVIUS

                                    So I hope.
I was not born to die on Brutus' sword.

BRUTUS

O if thou wert the noblest of thy strain,
Young man, thou couldst not die more honorable.

CASSIUS

60   A peevish schoolboy, worthless of such honor,
Joined with a masker and a reveler.

ANTONY

35   But not without their sting.

BRUTUS

    O yes, and without sound either,
    because you have stolen their buzzing, Antony,
    and very wisely make threats before you sting.

ANTONY

    Villains, you didn't even do that when your vile daggers
40   hacked one another in Caesar's body.
    You grinned like apes, and were servile like hounds,
    and bowed like slaves, kissing Caesar's feet,
    while damned Casca, like a cur, from behind
    struck Caesar on the neck. O you flatterers!

CASSIUS

45   Flatterers? Now, Brutus, you have only yourself to thank.
    This tongue of Antony could not be so offensive today
    if Cassius had prevailed (and Antony had been killed
       with Caesar).

OCTAVIUS

    Come, come, let's get down to business. If this argument
       makes us sweat,
    settling it by the sword will turn our sweat into bloody drops.
50   Look here, I draw a sword against conspirators.
    When do you think I will sheathe my sword again?
    Not until Caesar's thirty-three wounds
    be well avenged, or until you kill Octavius Caesar
    and add another slaughter to your traitorous swords.

BRUTUS

55   Caesar, you can't die at the hands of traitors
    unless you kill yourself with your own hands.

OCTAVIUS

    That's what I hope.
    I was not born to die on Brutus's sword.

BRUTUS

    O even if you were the noblest of all your family,
    young man, you could not die more honorably.

CASSIUS (*to Brutus*)

60   He's a childish schoolboy, unworthy of such an honor,
    joined with Antony, who is only a masquerader and a party-goer.

ANTONY
    Old Cassius still.

OCTAVIUS
                        Come, Antony. Away!
    Defiance, traitors, hurl we in your teeth.
    If you dare fight today, come to the field;
65   If not, when you have stomachs.
                Exit OCTAVIUS, ANTONY, *and Army*.

CASSIUS
    Why, now, blow wind, swell billow, and swim bark.
    The storm is up, and all is on the hazard.

BRUTUS
    Ho, Lucilius, hark, a word with you.
            LUCILIUS *stands forth*.

LUCILIUS
                                My lord?
            [BRUTUS *and* LUCILIUS *speak apart*.]

CASSIUS
    Messala.
            MESSALA *stands forth*.

MESSALA
                What says my general?

CASSIUS
                                Messala,
70   This is my birthday; as this very day
    Was Cassius born. Give me thy hand, Messala.
    Be thou my witness that against my will,
    As Pompey was, am I compelled to set
    Upon one battle all our liberties.
75   You know that I held Epicurus* strong,
    And his opinion. Now I change my mind,
    And partly credit things that do presage.
    Coming from Sardis, on our former ensign
    Two mighty eagles fell, and there they perched,
80   Gorging and feeding from our soldiers' hands,
    Who to Philippi here consorted us.
    This morning are they fled away and gone,

---

    75 *Epicurus* The Epicurean philosophy was strongly materialistic a
    assumed that the gods do not trouble themselves about human affairs. Om
    and portents, therefore, are of no significance and should be ignored.

ANTONY

The same old Cassius.

OCTAVIUS

Come, Antony. Let's go!

We hurl defiance, traitors, in your faces.

If you dare to fight today, come to the battlefield;

65 if not, come when you have the stomach for it.

Exit OCTAVIUS, ANTONY, *and their army.*

CASSIUS

Why, now, let the wind blow, the ocean wave swell, and our ship swim on the water.

The storm has begun, and we have risked all (on this throw of the dice).

BRUTUS

Lucilius, listen, may I have a word with you.

LUCILIUS *comes up to* BRUTUS.

LUCILIUS

My lord?

BRUTUS *and* LUCILIUS *speak to each other at one side of the stage.*

CASSIUS

Messala.

MESSALA *comes up to* CASSIUS.

MESSALA

What says my general?

CASSIUS

Messala,

70 today is my birthday; on this very day

Cassius was born. Give me your hand, Messala.

Be my witness that—against my will,

as Pompey was—I am forced to risk

all our freedoms in one battle.

75 You know that I used to believe strongly in Epicurus

and his opinions. Now I change my mind,

and partly believe in omens that foretell the future.

Coming from Sardis, I saw two mighty eagles swoop down

on our foremost banner,

and there they perched,

80 feeding and gorging themselves from our soldiers' hands.

Those eagles accompanied us to Philippi.

This morning they have fled away and gone,

And in their steads do ravens, crows, and kites
Fly o'er our heads and downward look on us
85   As we were sickly prey. Their shadows seem
A canopy most fatal, under which
Our army lies, ready to give up the ghost.

MESSALA
Believe not so.

CASSIUS
                              I but believe it partly,
For I am fresh of spirit and resolved
90   To meet all perils very constantly.

BRUTUS
Even so, Lucilius.

CASSIUS
                              Now, most noble Brutus,
The gods today stand friendly, that we may,
Lovers in peace, lead on our days to age.
But since the affairs of men rests still incertain,
95   Let's reason with the worst that may befall.
If we do lose this battle, then is this
The very last time we shall speak together.
What are you then determinèd to do?

BRUTUS
Even by the rule of that philosophy
100   By which I did blame Cato* for the death
Which he did give himself—I know not how,
But I do find it cowardly and vile,
For fear of what might fall, so to prevent
The time of life—arming myself with patience
105   To stay the providence of some high powers
That govern us below.

CASSIUS
                              Then, if we lose this battle,
You are contented to be led in triumph
Thorough the streets of Rome?

BRUTUS
No, Cassius, no. Think not, thou noble Roman,
110   That ever Brutus will go bound to Rome;

---

100 *Cato*   Marcus Cato, Portia's father, who, after the defeat of Pompey
at Pharsalia, fought on and finally killed himself at Utica in 46 B.C. rather
than submit to Caesar. See note at 2.1.295.

and in their place, ravens, crows, and scavenging hawks
   (all birds of bad omen),
fly over our heads and look down on us
as if we were sick and waiting to be their prey.
   Their shadows seem
like a deadly canopy, under which
our army lies, ready to die.

MESSALA
   Don't believe it.

CASSIUS
   I only partly believe it,
because my spirit is fresh and I am resolved
to meet all perils with determination.

BRUTUS (*concluding his conversation with Lucilius*)
   Right, Lucilius.

CASSIUS
   Now, most noble Brutus,
may the gods today be well-disposed to us, so that we may,
as good friends in peace, lead our lives on to old age.
But since the affairs of men always remain doubtful,
let's assume that the worst may happen.
If we lose this battle, then this is
the very last time that we shall speak together.
What are you then resolved to do?

BRUTUS
   Even by the rules of the Stoic philosophy
by which I blamed Cato for the death
which he gave himself—I don't know why,
but I find it cowardly and vile,
for fear of being dishonored, to shorten by suicide
the natural limit of life—I will arm myself with patience
to await the will of those high gods
that govern us here on earth.

CASSIUS
   Then, if we lose this battle,
you are contented to be led in triumph
through the streets of Rome (i.e., as a captive in a
   victory procession)?

BRUTUS
   No, Cassius, no. Don't believe, you noble Roman,
that Brutus will ever go to Rome as a bound captive—

He bears too great a mind. But this same day
Must end that work the ides of March begun.
And whether we shall meet again I know not;
Therefore our everlasting farewell take:
115   For ever and for ever farewell, Cassius.
If we do meet again, why, we shall smile;
If not, why then this parting was well made.

CASSIUS
For ever and for ever farewell, Brutus.
If we do meet again, we'll smile indeed;
120   If not, 'tis true this parting was well made.

BRUTUS
Why then, lead on. O that a man might know
The end of this day's business ere it come!
But it sufficeth that the day will end,
And then the end is known. Come, ho! Away!
    Exeunt.

[*Scene ii: Near Philippi; the field of battle.*] *Alarum. Enter* BRUTU
and MESSALA.

BRUTUS
Ride, ride, Messala, ride, and give these bills
Unto the legions on the other side.
    Loud alarum.
Let them set on at once; for I perceive
But cold demeanor in Octavio's wing,
5   And sudden push gives them the overthrow.
Ride, ride, Messala; let them all come down.
    Exeunt.

[*Scene iii: Another part of the field.*] *Alarums. Enter* CASSIUS *a*
TITINIUS.

CASSIUS
O look, Titinius, look, the villains fly!
Myself have to mine own turned enemy.
This ensign here of mine was turning back;
I slew the coward, and did take it from him.

he has too great a sense of decency. But this very day
must end that enterprise begun on the ides of March.
And whether we shall meet again I know not;
therefore let us take our everlasting farewell of each other:
115   forever and forever farewell, Cassius.
If we happen to meet again, why, we shall smile;
if not, why then it was right for us to take leave of each other.
CASSIUS
Forever and forever farewell, Brutus.
If we happen to meet again, we'll smile indeed;
if not, it's true that it was right for us to take leave of
120   each other.
BRUTUS
Why, then, lead our armies on. O if a man might know
in advance
how this day's business would turn out!
But we must be satisfied that the day will end,
and then the result is known. Come! Let's move on!
     They exit.

Scene ii: Near Philippi; the battlefield. A call to arms is played on drums and trumpets. Enter BRUTUS *and* MESSALA.

BRUTUS
Ride, ride, Messala, ride, and give these orders
to the troops on the other side of the battlefield.
     Loud call to arms.
Let them move forward at once, because I perceive
a lack of fighting spirit in the army of Octavius,
5   and a sudden attack will defeat them.
Ride, ride, Messala. Let all the troops come down.
     They exit.

Scene iii: Another part of the battlefield. Calls to arms. Enter CASSIUS *and* TITINIUS.

CASSIUS
O look, Titinius, look! My cowardly troops are fleeing!
I have become the enemy of my own soldiers.
My flag-bearer here was turning back;
I killed the coward and took the flag away from him.

TITINIUS

5   O Cassius, Brutus gave the word too early,
Who, having some advantage on Octavius,
Took it too eagerly. His soldiers fell to spoil,
Whilst we by Antony are all enclosed.

       Enter PINDARUS.

PINDARUS

Fly further off, my lord, fly further off;
10   Mark Antony is in your tents, my lord.
Fly, therefore, noble Cassius, fly far off.

CASSIUS

This hill is far enough. Look, look, Titinius.
Are those my tents where I perceive the fire?

TITINIUS

They are, my lord.

CASSIUS

               Titinius, if thou lovest me,
15   Mount thou my horse, and hide thy spurs in him
Till he have brought thee up to yonder troops
And here again, that I may rest assured
Whether yond troops are friend or enemy.

TITINIUS

I will be here again even with a thought.

      Exit.

CASSIUS

20   Go, Pindarus, get higher on that hill;
My sight was ever thick. Regard Titinius,
And tell me what thou not'st about the field.

     [*Exit* PINDARUS.]

This day I breathèd first: time is come round,
And where I did begin, there shall I end;
25   My life is run his compass. Sirrah, what news?

PINDARUS

(*Above*) O my lord!

CASSIUS

What news?

PINDARUS

Titinius is enclosèd round about
With horsemen that make to him on the spur;

TITINIUS
5   O Cassius, Brutus gave the order to attack too early,
     who, having a small advantage over Octavius,
     pressed it too far. Brutus's soldiers began looting
     at the very time that we are completely surrounded by Antony.
          Enter PINDARUS.

PINDARUS
     Retreat further off, my lord, retreat still further;
10   Mark Antony is in your tents, my lord.
     Retreat, therefore, noble Cassius, retreat further off.

CASSIUS
     This hill is far enough. Look, look, Titinius.
     Are those my tents that are on fire?

TITINIUS
     They are, my lord.

CASSIUS
     Titinius, if you love me,
15   mount my horse and spur him on with all possible speed
     until he has brought you to those troops there
     and back here again, that I may rest assured
     whether those troops are friend or foe.

TITINIUS
     I will be back again even with the speed of thought.
          Exit.

CASSIUS
20   Go, Pindarus, get up higher on that hill;
     my eyesight was always bad. Keep an eye on Titinius,
     and tell me what you observe about the battlefield.
          Exit PINDARUS.
     On this day I took my first breath. Time is come around,
     and where I began there shall I end;
25   my life has completed its full circle. Fellow, what's the news?

PINDARUS (*from the upper stage*)
     O my lord!

CASSIUS
     What news?

PINDARUS
     Titinius is enclosed all around
     by horsemen that approach him at full speed,

30   Yet he spurs on. Now they are almost on him.
    Now, Titinius! Now some light. O he lights too!
    He's ta'en. (*Shout*) And hark, they shout for joy.

CASSIUS
    Come down; behold no more.
    O coward that I am to live so long
35   To see my best friend ta'en before my face.

       Enter PINDARUS.

    Come hither, sirrah.
    In Parthia did I take thee prisoner;
    And then I swore thee, saving of thy life,
    That whatsoever I did bid thee do,
40   Thou shouldst attempt it. Come now, keep thine oath;
    Now be a freeman, and with this good sword
    That ran through Caesar's bowels, search this bosom.
    Stand not,to answer. Here, take thou the hilts;
    And when my face is covered, as 'tis now,
45   Guide thou the sword.—Caesar, thou art revenged,
    Even with the sword that killed thee.

       [*Dies.*]

PINDARUS
    So, I am free; yet would not so have been,
    Durst I have done my will. O Cassius!
    Far from this country Pindarus shall run,
50   Where never Roman shall take note of him.

       [*Exit.*]
       Enter TITINIUS *and* MESSALA.

MESSALA
    It is but change, Titinius; for Octavius
    Is overthrown by noble Brutus' power,
    As Cassius' legions are by Antony.

TITINIUS
    These tidings will well comfort Cassius.

MESSALA
    Where did you leave him?

TITINIUS
                    All disconsolate,
55   With Pindarus his bondman, on this hill.

    yet he spurs on. Now they are almost on top of him.

    Go on, Titinius! Now some dismount. O he dismounts too!

    He's taken. (*Shout*) And listen, they shout for joy.

CASSIUS

    Come down; don't look any more.

    O what a coward I am to live so long

    to see my best friend captured before my face.

        Enter PINDARUS.

    Come here, fellow.

    In Parthia I took you prisoner,

    and then I made you swear that, having spared your life,

    whatever I ordered you to do,

    you would try to do it. Come now, keep your oath.

    Now make yourself a free man, and with this good sword

    that ran through Caesar's guts, pierce my own chest.

    Don't stand about thinking of an answer. Here, take the hilt

       of my sword,

    and when my face is covered, as it is now,

    guide the sword. (*Pindarus stabs Cassius.*) Caesar,

       you are revenged,

    with the same sword that I used to kill you.

        Dies.

PINDARUS

    So, now I am free, yet I would not have been

    if I had dared to do what I wanted to (i.e., refused to kill

       Cassius). O Cassius!

    Far from this country shall Pindarus run,

    where no Roman shall ever take notice of him.

        Exit.

        Enter TITINIUS *and* MESSALA.

MESSALA

    It is only an even exchange, Titinius, because Octavius

    was defeated by the noble Brutus's army,

    while Cassius's legions were vanquished by Antony.

TITINIUS

    This news will please Cassius very much.

MESSALA

    Where did you leave him?

TITINIUS

    Very dejected,

    with his slave Pindarus, on this hill.

MESSALA
Is not that he that lies upon the ground?

TITINIUS
He lies not like the living. O my heart!

MESSALA
Is not that he?

TITINIUS
                    No, this was he, Messala,
60   But Cassius is no more. O setting sun,
As in thy red rays thou dost sink to night,
So in his red blood Cassius' day is set.
The sun of Rome is set. Our day is gone;
Clouds, dews, and dangers come; our deeds are done.
65   Mistrust of my success hath done this deed.

MESSALA
Mistrust of good success hath done this deed.
O hateful Error, Melancholy's child,*
Why dost thou show to the apt thoughts of men
The things that are not? O Error, soon conceived,
70   Thou never com'st unto a happy birth,
But kill'st the mother that engend'red thee.

TITINIUS
What, Pindarus! Where art thou, Pindarus?

MESSALA
Seek him, Titinius, whilst I go to meet
The noble Brutus, thrusting this report
75   Into his ears. I may say thrusting it;
For piercing steel and darts envenomèd
Shall be as welcome to the ears of Brutus
As tidings of this sight.

TITINIUS
                    Hie you, Messala,
And I will seek for Pindarus the while.
        [*Exit* MESSALA.]
80   Why didst thou send me forth, brave Cassius?
Did I not meet thy friends, and did not they
Put on my brows this wreath of victory,
And bid me give it thee? Didst thou not hear their shouts?
Alas, thou hast misconstrued everything.*

---

67 *Error, Melancholy's child* a fanciful genealogy intended to connect Cassius's death with his gloomy, fatalistic mood. These formal, elaborate personifications occur frequently in *Julius Caesar*, and they are used to make an allegorical comparison.

84 *misconstrued everything* Cassius, whose "sight was ever thick" (5.3. 21), has completely misunderstood what happened with Titinius earlier in this scene. As Titinius explains the events to us, he was welcomed by the

MESSALA

   Is not that Cassius who lies on the ground?

TITINIUS

   He does not lie like someone who's alive. O keep my heart
      from breaking!

MESSALA

   Is not that he?

TITINIUS

   No, this *was* he, Messala,

60   but Cassius is no longer alive. O setting sun,
   just as you sink down into night in your red rays,
   so in his red blood has Cassius's life set.
   The sun of Rome has set. Our day is over;
   let clouds, harmful dews, and dangers now approach; our deeds
      are done.

65   Distrust about the outcome of my mission has caused
      Cassius's death.

MESSALA

   Distrust about a good outcome has done this deed.
   O hateful Error, the child of Melancholy,
   why, to the ready thoughts of men, do you present
   false appearances? O Error, quickly conceived,

70   you don't ever come to a happy birth,
   but kill the mother that gave you life.

TITINIUS

   Come here, Pindarus! Where are you, Pindarus?

MESSALA

   Seek him out, Titinius, while I go to meet
   the noble Brutus, and thrust this bad news

75   into his ears. I may say "thrust" it,
   since piercing steel and poisoned arrows
   will be as welcome to the ears of Brutus
   as my account of this pitiful sight.

TITINIUS

   Go quickly, Messala,
   and, in the meantime, I will look for Pindarus.
      Exit MESSALA.

80   Why did you send me on that mission, brave Cassius?
   Did I not meet your friends, and did they not
   put on my head this wreath of victory,
   and order me to give it to you? Did you not hear their shouts?
   Alas, you have misinterpreted everything.

---

troops of Brutus, who had won a victory over Octavius. The report that
Pindarus gives Cassius from his lookout post is, of course, misleading,
especially the information that Titinius is "taken" (5.3.32). Cassius should
have verified this intelligence rather than committing suicide in despair. A
sense of fatality hangs over the conspirators, even when they are temporarily
victorious (as Brutus is over Octavius).

85   But hold thee, take this garland on thy brow;
Thy Brutus bid me give it thee, and I
Will do his bidding. Brutus, come apace,
And see how I regarded Caius Cassius.
By your leave, gods. This is a Roman's part.*

90   Come, Cassius' sword, and find Titinius' heart.

      Dies.
      Alarum. Enter BRUTUS, MESSALA, YOUNG CATO, STRATO, VOLUMNIUS, *and* LUCILIUS, [*with* LABIO, FLAVIUS, *and others*].

BRUTUS
    Where, where, Messala, doth his body lie?

MESSALA
    Lo, yonder, and Titinius mourning it.

BRUTUS
    Titinius' face is upward.

CATO
               He is slain.

BRUTUS
    O Julius Caesar, thou art mighty yet!

95   Thy spirit walks abroad and turns our swords
    In our own proper entrails.

      Low alarums.

CATO
               Brave Titinius!
    Look whe'r he have not crowned dead Cassius.

BRUTUS
    Are yet two Romans living such as these?
    The last of all the Romans, fare thee well.

100   It is impossible that ever Rome
    Should breed thy fellow. Friends, I owe moe tears
    To this dead man than you shall see me pay.
    I shall find time, Cassius; I shall find time.
    Come, therefore, and to Tharsus send his body.

105   His funerals shall not be in our camp,
    Lest it discomfort us. Lucilius, come;
    And come, young Cato; let us to the field.
    Labio and Flavio set our battles on.

---

89 *Roman's part* The Roman view of suicide as a praiseworthy act, especially when it is done to avoid dishonor, is directly opposed to the Christian condemnation of suicide as a form of murder.

35 But wait a minute, let me put this victory garland on your brow.
Brutus wanted me to give it to you, and I
will do as he wished. Brutus, come quickly,
and see how much love I felt for Caius Cassius.
With your permission, O gods. Suicide is the proper part for
   a Roman to play now.

90 Come, Cassius's sword, and find Titinius's heart.
> *Dies.*
> *Call to arms. Enter* BRUTUS, MESSALA, YOUNG CATO,
> STRATO, VOLUMNIUS, *and* LUCILIUS, *with* LABIO,
> FLAVIUS, *and others.*

BRUTUS
Where, where, Messala, does Cassius's body lie?

MESSALA
Over there, and Titinius is mourning it.

BRUTUS
Titinius lies face upward.

CATO
Someone has killed him.

BRUTUS
O Julius Caesar, you are still mighty!
95 Your spirit walks about and turns our swords
into our own guts.
> *Low calls to arms.*

CATO
Brave Titinius!
Look, he has crowned dead Cassius.

BRUTUS
Are there still two Romans living such as Cassius and Titinius?
(*To the dead Cassius*) The last of all the Romans, farewell.
100 It is impossible that Rome should ever
give birth to your equal. (*To his followers*) Friends, I owe
   more tears
to this dead man than you shall see me pay.
I shall find time, Cassius; I shall find time.
Come, therefore, and send Cassius's body to Tarsus.
105 His funeral shall not be in our camp
for fear that it will depress our troops. Lucilius, come;
and come, young Cato; let us go to the battlefield.
Labio and Flavio, let's advance with our forces.

'Tis three a clock; and, Romans, yet ere night
110   We shall try fortune in a second fight.
    Exeunt.

[*Scene iv: Another part of the field.*] *Alarum. Enter* BRUTUS
MESSALA, [YOUNG] CATO, LUCILIUS, *and* FLAVIUS.

BRUTUS
    Yet, countrymen, O yet hold up your heads!
        [*Exit, with* MESSALA *and* FLAVIUS.]
[YOUNG] CATO
    What bastard doth not? Who will go with me?
    I will proclaim my name about the field.
    I am the son of Marcus Cato,* ho!
5   A foe to tyrants, and my country's friend.
    I am the son of Marcus Cato, ho!
        Enter Soldiers and fight.
[LUCILIUS]
    And I am Brutus, Marcus Brutus, I!
    Brutus, my country's friend! Know me for Brutus!
        [YOUNG CATO *is slain.*]
    O young and noble Cato, art thou down?
10   Why, now thou diest as bravely as Titinius,
    And mayst be honored, being Cato's son.
[FIRST] SOLDIER
    Yield, or thou diest.
LUCILIUS
               Only I yield to die.
    There is so much that thou wilt kill me straight:
    Kill Brutus, and be honored in his death.
[FIRST] SOLDIER
15   We must not; a noble prisoner.
        Enter ANTONY.
SECOND SOLDIER
    Room, ho! Tell Antony Brutus is ta'en.
FIRST SOLDIER
    I'll tell the news. Here comes the general.
    Brutus is ta'en, Brutus is ta'en, my lord.

---

   4 *Marcus Cato* see notes at 2.1.295 and 5.1.100. Young Cato is the
brother of Portia, Brutus's wife.

It's three o'clock, and, Romans, once more before nightfall
10   we shall try our luck in a second fight.
    They exit.

Scene iv: Another part of the battlefield. Call to arms. Enter
BRUTUS, MESSALA, YOUNG CATO, LUCILIUS, *and* FLAVIUS.

BRUTUS (*encouraging his troops*)
  Once more, my countrymen, O still hold up your heads!
    Exit, with MESSALA *and* FLAVIUS.

YOUNG CATO
  Who is of such base blood (i.e., not a true-born Roman) that he
    wouldn't? Who will go with me?
  I will shout out my name about the battlefield.
  I am the son of Marcus Cato, that's right!
5   An enemy to tyrants and my country's friend.
  I am the son of Marcus Cato, that's right!
    Enter Soldiers and fight.

LUCILIUS (*impersonating Brutus*)
  And I am Brutus, Marcus Brutus, I!
  Brutus, my country's friend! Know that I am Brutus!
    YOUNG CATO *is killed.*
  O young and noble Cato, are you down?
10   Why, now you die as bravely as Titinius,
  and may be honored, being Cato's son.

FIRST SOLDIER
  Surrender or you die.

LUCILIUS
  I will surrender only when you kill me.
  When you know who I am, you will want to kill me immediately:
  kill Brutus and win glory by his death.

FIRST SOLDIER
15   We must not; he is a noble prisoner.
    Enter ANTONY.

SECOND SOLDIER
  Make room there! Tell Antony that Brutus is captured.

FIRST SOLDIER
  I'll tell the news. Here comes the general.
  Brutus is captured, Brutus is captured, my lord.

ANTONY

Where is he?

LUCILIUS

20   Safe, Antony; Brutus is safe enough.
       I dare assure thee that no enemy
       Shall ever take alive the noble Brutus.
       The gods defend him from so great a shame.
       When you do find him, or alive or dead,
25   He will be found like Brutus, like himself.

ANTONY

       This is not Brutus, friend; but, I assure you,
       A prize no less in worth. Keep this man safe;
       Give him all kindness. I had rather have
       Such men my friends than enemies. Go on,
30   And see whe'r Brutus be alive or dead;
       And bring us word unto Octavius' tent
       How every thing is chanced.
              Exeunt.

[*Scene v: Another part of the field.*] *Enter* BRUTUS, DARDANIU
CLITUS, STRATO, *and* VOLUMNIUS.

BRUTUS

       Come, poor remains of friends, rest on this rock.

CLITUS

       Statilius showed the torchlight; but, my lord,
       He came not back. He is or ta'en or slain.*

BRUTUS

       Sit thee down, Clitus. Slaying is the word;
5   It is a deed in fashion. Hark thee, Clitus.
            [*Whispers.*]

CLITUS

       What, I, my lord? No, not for all the world.

---

3 *slain* Plutarch relates that Statilius, as scout, went through the e
emy's lines to Cassius's camp and gave a prearranged signal by torchlig
that all was well. He was, however, slain on his way back to Brutus.

ANTONY
>Where is he?

LUCILIUS
20
>Safe, Antony; Brutus is safe enough.
>I dare assure you that no enemy
>shall ever take the noble Brutus alive.
>May the gods defend him from so great a disgrace.
>When you find him, either alive or dead,
25
>he will always behave like Brutus: true to his own noble nature.

ANTONY
>This is not Brutus, my friend, but, I assure you,
>a prize of no less value. Keep this man safe;
>treat him with all military courtesy. I had rather have
>such men as my friends than as my enemies. Go on before us,
30
>and see whether Brutus is alive or dead,
>and bring me word to Octavius's tent
>how everything has turned out.
>>*They exit.*

Scene v: Another part of the battlefield. Enter BRUTUS, DAR-
DANIUS, CLITUS, STRATO, *and* VOLUMNIUS.

BRUTUS
>Come, you who are left of my friends, let's rest on this rock.

CLITUS
>Statilius gave the signal by the light of his torch, but, my lord,
>he didn't come back. He is either captured or killed.

BRUTUS
>Sit down, Clitus. Killing is the word we keep hearing;
5
>it is now a fashionable deed. Listen to me, Clitus.
>>*Whispers.*

CLITUS
>What, I, my lord? No, I wouldn't do it for all the world.

BRUTUS
Peace then, no words.

CLITUS
                    I'll rather kill myself.

BRUTUS
Hark thee, Dardanius.
     [*Whispers.*]

DARDANIUS
                    Shall I do such a deed?

CLITUS
O Dardanius!

DARDANIUS
10   O Clitus!

CLITUS
What ill request did Brutus make to thee?

DARDANIUS
To kill him, Clitus. Look, he meditates.

CLITUS
Now is that noble vessel full of grief,
That it runs over even at his eyes.

BRUTUS
15   Come hither, good Volumnius; list a word.

VOLUMNIUS
What says my lord?

BRUTUS
                    Why this, Volumnius.
The ghost of Caesar hath appeared to me
Two several times by night: at Sardis once,
And this last night here in Philippi fields.
I know my hour is come.

VOLUMNIUS
20   Not so, my lord.

BRUTUS
Nay, I am sure it is, Volumnius.
Thou seest the world, Volumnius, how it goes;
Our enemies have beat us to the pit.
     Low alarums.
It is more worthy to leap in ourselves
25   Than tarry till they push us. Good Volumnius,
Thou know'st that we two went to school together.

BRUTUS
Silence then—no words.

CLITUS
I'd rather kill myself.

BRUTUS
Listen to me, Dardanius.
Whispers.

DARDANIUS
Do you really want me to do such a deed?

CLITUS
O Dardanius!

DARDANIUS
O Clitus!

CLITUS
What evil request did Brutus make of you?

DARDANIUS
To kill him, Clitus. Look, he is thinking.

CLITUS
Now is Brutus like a noble vessel so full of grief
that it runs over in tears at his eyes.

BRUTUS
Come here, good Volumnius; let me have a word with you.

VOLUMNIUS
What says my lord?

BRUTUS
Why this, Volumnius.
The ghost of Caesar has appeared to me
two separate times at night: at Sardis once
and last night here in the fields of Philippi.
I know that my hour of death has come.

VOLUMNIUS
That's not true, my lord.

BRUTUS
No, I am sure it has, Volumnius.
You see how things are, Volumnius, how our luck is going.
Our enemies have beaten us to the edge of our graves.
Low calls to arms.
It is nobler to leap in ourselves
than wait until they push us. Good Volumnius,
you remember that we both went to school together.

Even for that our love of old, I prithee
Hold thou my sword-hilts whilst I run on it.

VOLUMNIUS

That's not an office for a friend, my lord.

Alarum still.

CLITUS

30   Fly, fly, my lord, there is no tarrying here.

BRUTUS

Farewell to you; and you; and you, Volumnius.
Strato, thou hast been all this while asleep.
Farewell to thee too, Strato. Countrymen,
My heart doth joy that yet in all my life
35   I found no man but he was true to me.
I shall have glory by this losing day
More than Octavius and Mark Antony
By this vile conquest shall attain unto.
So fare you well at once; for Brutus' tongue
40   Hath almost ended his life's history.
Night hangs upon mine eyes; my bones would rest,
That have but labored to attain this hour.

Alarum. Cry within, "Fly, fly, fly!"

CLITUS

Fly, my lord, fly!

BRUTUS

Hence! I will follow.

[Exeunt CLITUS, DARDANIUS, *and* VOLUMNIUS.]

I prithee, Strato, stay thou by thy lord.
45   Thou art a fellow of a good respect;
Thy life hath had some smatch of honor in it.
Hold then my sword, and turn away thy face,
While I do run upon it. Wilt thou, Strato?

STRATO

Give me your hand first. Fare you well, my lord.

BRUTUS

50   Farewell, good Strato. [*Runs on his sword.*] Caesar, now be still;
I killed not thee with half so good a will.

Dies.

Alarum. Retreat. Enter ANTONY, OCTAVIUS, MESSALA,
LUCILIUS, *and the Army.*

For the sake of our old friendship, I beg you
to hold my sword hilt while I run onto my sword.

VOLUMNIUS

That's not a task you can ask a friend to do, my lord.
Call to arms continues.

CLITUS

30 Flee, flee, my lord, you can't linger here.

BRUTUS

Farewell to you ; and you ; and you, Volumnius.
Strato, you have been asleep all this time.
Farewell to you too, Strato. Countrymen,
my heart rejoices that in all my life
35 I found no man who was not faithful and honest to me.
I shall have more glory from this day of defeat
than Octavius and Mark Antony
shall achieve from their vile conquest.
So fare you well all together, because Brutus's tongue
40 has almost concluded the history of his life.
My eyes are growing dim ; my bones would like to rest
that have been laboring all their life to reach this hour.
Call to arms. A cry off-stage, "Flee, flee, flee!"

CLITUS

Flee, my lord, flee !

BRUTUS

Go ahead ! I will follow.
Exit CLITUS, DARDANIUS, *and* VOLUMNIUS.
I beg of you, Strato, remain with your lord.
45 You are a fellow of good reputation ;
your life has had some taste of honor in it.
Hold my sword then, and turn your face away
while I run upon it. Will you, Strato?

STRATO

Give me your hand first. Farewell, my lord.

BRUTUS

50 Farewell, good Strato. (*Runs on his sword.*) Caesar, now your
ghost can rest in peace.
I did not kill you half so eagerly as I killed myself.
Dies.
Call to arms. Retreat sounded. Enter ANTONY, OCTA-
VIUS, LUCILIUS, *and the army.*

OCTAVIUS
What man is that?

MESSALA
My master's man. Strato, where is thy master?

STRATO
Free from the bondage you are in, Messala.
55 The conquerors can but make a fire of him;
For Brutus only overcame himself,
And no man else hath honor by his death.

LUCILIUS
So Brutus should be found. I thank thee, Brutus,
That thou hast proved Lucilius' saying true.*

OCTAVIUS
60 All that served Brutus, I will entertain them.
Fellow, wilt thou bestow thy time with me?

STRATO
Ay, if Messala will prefer me to you.

OCTAVIUS
Do so, good Messala.

MESSALA
How died my master, Strato?

STRATO
65 I held the sword, and he did run on it.

MESSALA
Octavius, then take him to follow thee,
That did the latest service to my master.

ANTONY
This was the noblest Roman of them all.
All the conspirators save only he
70 Did that they did in envy of great Caesar;
He only, in a general honest thought
And common good to all, made one of them.
His life was gentle, and the elements
So mixed in him that Nature might stand up
75 And say to all the world, "This was a man!"

---

59 *true*   see 5.4.21-25.

OCTAVIUS
What man is that?

MESSALA
My master's servant. Strato, where is your master?

STRATO
Free from the slavery you are in, Messala.
The victors can only cremate his body (i.e., not capture
55   him alive),
because Brutus alone conquered himself,
and no one else has won glory by his death.

LUCILIUS
That's the kind of honorable act we expected from Brutus.
    I thank you, Brutus,
because you have proved true what I said about you.

OCTAVIUS
60   All those who served Brutus I will take into my service.
Fellow, will you join with me?

STRATO
Yes, if Messala will recommend me to you.

OCTAVIUS
Do so, good Messala.

MESSALA
How did Brutus die, Strato?

STRATO
65   I held the sword and he ran onto it.

MESSALA
Octavius, then take him as your follower,
who did the ultimate service for my master.

ANTONY (*speaking a formal eulogy for the dead Brutus*)
This was the noblest Roman of them all.
All the conspirators, except Brutus,
70   did what they did out of jealousy and spite against great Caesar.
Only Brutus joined them for public, honorable motives
and concern for the common good of the Roman people.
His life was noble and the elements of his character were
so harmoniously mixed that Nature might stand up
75   and declare to the whole world, "This was a man!"

OCTAVIUS
    According to his virtue let us use him,
    With all respect and rites of burial.
    Within my tent his bones tonight shall lie,
    Most like a soldier, ordered honorably.
80   So call the field to rest, and let's away
    To part the glories of this happy day.
        Exeunt omnes.

OCTAVIUS
    Let us deal with him according to his great worth,
    and render him all due respect and proper rites of burial.
    Within my tent his body shall lie tonight,
    like a soldier, and be treated with all appropriate honors.
80   Let us recall our armies to rest, and let's leave here
    to share the glories of this most fortunate day.
      All exit.

THE PLAY IN REVIEW:

A Teacher and Student Supplement

Between Acts: Study Questions

Act I

1. What is the purpose of the interchange between Marullus and the commoners?

    The play opens at a holiday, and the boisterousness of the setting creates an atmosphere of excitement and anticipation of great events. The nature of these events — based on popular acceptance of Caesar contrasting the discontent of a small but effectively organized group — is exposed in Marullus' denunciation of the cobbler for forgetting Pompey's death and honoring Caesar. This speech foreshadows words Mark Antony will use in the funeral oration for Caesar himself, words marking the contrast between love and gratitude. Finally, these commoners, unimportant as individuals, typify "the mob," later an essential collective character in the drama.

2. How are Antony and Brutus contrasted as each appears for the first time?

    Antony appears as totally subject to Caesar, a devoted follower, a position he maintains until he has avenged his idol's death. Still, even in this initial presentation as disciple of a greater man, he is shown as a mover, a man of action, symbolized by the fact that he is brought on stage shortly before he is about to begin a run. Brutus, a more reflective type, is introduced in a contemplative mood. He tends to stand aside and consider, rather than rush into action. In this respect he understands himself: he acknowledges immediately that he lacks some of that "quick spirit" which Antony possesses. He fails to envision the outcome of that lack. Antony is later quick to seize his advantage and win his victory, while Brutus is forever slow to come to

196

a decision. When he does, it is usually a wrong decision.

3. How is Cassius characterized?

He is a manipulator, a user of others, but a keen judge of human nature. Because his respect for Brutus is tinged with contempt, he knows just the sort of flattery which will achieve his ends. However, he hypocritically denies using such a base tool. He unwittingly reveals his own envious spite toward Caesar ("And this man is now become a god, and Cassius is a wretched creature") but masks it with devotion to Rome; he counts on Brutus' heritage of opposition to tyranny to win him over. In this way he uses the best within Brutus to support the worst within himself.

4. What thematic statement is voiced by Cassius in Scene 2?

The famous lines "The fault, dear Brutus, is not in our stars, But in ourselves" contain Shakespeare's belief that men are not helpless pawns of destiny but self-determining humans who forge their own fates. Cassius is urging Brutus to act, to make a moral stand. The irony is that in so doing Brutus sets into action forces which will destroy him.

5. What qualities appear in Caesar?

Caesar, whose name is the title of the play, is not the protagonist, that main character whose decisions and actions determine the outcome of the action. That role falls to Brutus. Caesar, however, is a fit ruler and superb leader, yet a man for all his power. He is shrewd, as shown by his estimate of Cassius, and supremely arrogant about his powers. Perhaps, hints Shakespeare, there is some foundation for the conspirators' fears of his ambition. Even with all his pride and virtue, he is flawed by human frailty. He is an aging man, cursed with partial deafness and the "falling sickness," worried about a barren wife. This combination of factors is a reminder that all men, no matter how powerful, eventually fall victim to their human condition.

6. **What is the irony of Casca's description of the populace?**

He sees them as "tag-rag people," the "common herd," yet it is the rights of these lowly people that the conspirators ostensibly hope to protect. Casca's comments reveal the duplicity of the conspiracy; it is not democracy in the sense of popular rule that they want to preserve, but their own rights and powers. Only Brutus is free of the jealousy of Caesar which motivates the others, though they mask it by references to the good of Rome. And Brutus is blind to their duplicity. Also important in Casca's description of the crowd's loyalty to Caesar is a foreshadowing of the role mob emotion will play in the resolution of the conflict.

7. **What metaphor dominates Cassius' estimate of Brutus?**

Cassius speaks several times of Brutus in terms of "metal." When Brutus tells him he will consider the conspirators' ideas, Cassius says he is glad his words have "struck but thus much show of fire from Brutus." Now he says "Thy honourable metal may be wrought." Brutus, whose honor seems stiff and immovable as metal, can be molded by someone who — like a smithy — knows how to manipulate the material at hand. Cassius believes himself such an artisan. This metaphor was also the basis for a pun, a play on words dear to the Elizabethans and masterfully devised by Shakespeare. For the "metal" of which Brutus is composed is also his "mettle," his basic spirit. It is this which Cassius intends to shape to his own ends.

8. **Why are the supernatural happenings reported in Scene 3?**

These are omens, and the superstitious Elizabethans expected such phenomena in a drama. More important, however, was the "great chain of being"; the audience believed the universe was completely and comprehensively organized, like a machine, with everything having a particular place and function. As long as each component, be it animal or man, kept to its fixed position, harmony would reign. Memories of civil strife intensified the sixteenth century's love of order, and they insisted on an interdependence of all parts. As God was to the world, so was the sun to the heavens, the king to the nations. If one of these primacies should be overthrown, as the conspirators intend, the rest must follow it to chaos: if a subject should kill a king, then an owl might attack the falcon, and a wolf overthrow the lion. Obedience, respect, degree, and status were the forms in which men stated their belief that the chain of being must be preserved. Because of the new security of Tudor England after a long history of civil wars, disruption of order in the chain of being was considered a most heinous crime. The assassination of a monarch would strike a blow against the entire universe. When the conspirators' plot is ready, it is not surprising that all nature cries out in protest — that storms roar, lightning strikes, and ghostly phenomena plague the streets. These horrors would be accepted by the Elizabethans as nature's protest against the imminence of disruption in the human sphere.

9. **What is revealed in Cassius' rebuke to Casca?**

His duplicity is underscored when he calls Casca "dull," a word he had specifically denied in Brutus' estimate of the man. Apparently, he knows Casca for what he is but continues to use him as he can, just as he hopes to use Brutus.

10. **What ideas emerge from Cassius' reflections on Caesar in Scene 3?**

Again, he bares his own envy of Caesar, once his equal, now his superior. He tries to deny the omens and Caesar's greatness by equating the frightening but generally ineffective storm to Caesar's vulnerable glory, a glory which can be extinguished by assassination. Cassius also muses that, like all men, he himself has the power to escape tyranny — by suicide, if all else fails — a foreshadowing of his death.

11. **Why does Casca use the word "alchemy" in assessing the value of Brutus to the conspiracy?**

In the continued "metal" imagery, alchemy was the age-old attempt to find a magic process for changing lead to gold. The conspirators hope that Brutus' outstanding public image will camouflage the nature of the assassination and make it acceptable to the Roman people. Unfortunately, they forget that alchemy was never successfully performed. Lead remains lead, a base metal, and murder remains murder, a base act.

Act II

12. Why is Brutus' speech at the beginning of Act II considered sincere?

It is a soliloquy and, in the Elizabethan theater, a soliloquy is a method of revealing a character's inner thoughts. What he says may not be truth in fact, but it expresses the truth as he sees it. In this soliloquy, Brutus assesses the political situation in Rome and decides his personal course of action. The whole speech is conditional, argument by analogy, comparing unlike things to find likenesses. His reasoning is particularly noteworthy as a means of self-justification. He holds no personal resentment against Caesar. He does find seemingly objective reasons for his leader's death and decides to do it "honestly," openly, letting the populace judge the action. The anonymous letters which reinforce his determination have been faked by Cassius; they symbolize the shaky ground on which Brutus bases his faith. Having convinced himself of the rightness of his decision, Brutus the idealist fails to visualize the outcome of his action.

13. What is Brutus' attitude toward the conspirators?

He has committed himself to their cause but cannot truly share their attitude. The subterfuge of their arrival disgusts him and he would prefer all action to be open. The desire to commit an immoral act in moral fashion is a contradiction in terms, an impossibility that reveals Brutus' ineptitude and creates the first of many clashes within the group. Brutus, with that inability to understand the realities of political action, denies the need of a binding oath. He tries to convince the others that the virtue of their intention is bond enough; he must somehow endow their intended action with an aura of goodness. By the end of their meeting he has assumed some of the attitudes inherent in their proposed deed and takes leave of them with the admonition that they hide their true intentions behind a jovial facade. This is part of Shakespeare's frequent reference to the difference between appearance and reality.

14. **What is the irony in the clash over Antony's death?**

Brutus refuses to allow the murder of Antony, who seems to him harmless. He forgets that Caesar too had seemed harmless, but that the need for preventive action convinced him otherwise. In this case, Cassius is pragmatically correct; for the conspiracy to succeed, Caesar's chief lieutenant must die with him. But Brutus has his way. Cassius must pay a heavy price — a series of tactical errors — for the prestige which Brutus brings to their cause.

15. **What does the scene with Portia reveal?**

This scene is intended to portray Brutus as the affectionate, solicitous husband, showing him as the noble man he is. His choice of wife compliments him: Portia is Cato's daughter, a bright and loving woman. Brutus' loving concern for Portia stresses the fine qualities of this man betrayed by his own weakness. In throwing his lot in with the conspirators Brutus is risking everything — love, honour, country, finally his very life. His plea of illness, not intended to be taken literally by the audience, reinforces his claim that Caesar's expanding power is a threat to Roman democracy.

16. **What is the purpose of Brutus' interview with Ligarius?**

The illness which he has used as an excuse to placate Portia is revealed as his concern for Rome under the rule of Caesar; Brutus views the state as an organism invaded by disease and tells Ligarius that he plans a deed which "will make sick men whole." Brutus truly believes in the moral justification of the assassination. Ligarius' readiness to accept the idea because it comes from Brutus bears witness to Cassius' shrewd planning. Brutus' involvement in the plot will render it palatable to many.

17. **What is the purpose of the conversation between Calpurnia and Caesar?**

Juxtaposed with the scene between Brutus and Portia, it shows Caesar and Brutus as much alike. Both are good men, yet one will soon be involved in the murder of the other. They are alike in their vulnerability to manipulation by others, for Decius Brutus has no more trouble manipulating Caesar than Cassius has with Brutus. Although Shakespeare has presented his philosophy of man's stake in his own destiny, Caesar here acts as a reminder that some aspects of destiny are above human power. He presents a fatalistic point of view: What will happen will happen. Also, Calpurnia's horror of the omens is a dramatic foreshadowing of the bloody killing to come, a continuation of tension of much import to the Elizabethans.

Several sides of Caesar's character are delineated. His kindness and affection for his wife are genuine, and he almost decides not to go to the Senate that day. Yet when Decius Brutus makes a clever appeal to his pride, he cannot resist it. His arrogance — Caesar must not be like other men — blinds him to the inescapable fact that Caesar is like other men. Like them, he is vulnerable.

18. **What ominous gathering closes Scene 2?**

The conspirators arrive to escort Caesar to the Senate. Their hypocritical politeness to him contrasts sharply with his pleasant, trusting welcome to them. Though Brutus remains firm in his resolution, he does so with self-reproach. The final words are Brutus', telling of his grief that though they may seem like friends, they are not really so. This provides grim counterpoint to the closing of the previous scene in which he has enjoined the other conspirators to hide the reality of their intentions behind a sham appearance. Now he mourns that appearance and reality cannot be the same.

19. **What is the purpose of Artemidorus' brief scene?**

This scene heightens the tension of the drama. Artemidorus functions as a device through which the outcome may be changed. But will he be able to reach Caesar in time? Suspense is prolonged and maintained at fever pitch.

20. **What is the effect of focusing upon Portia in Scene 4?**

First, putting the emphasis on Portia is a reminder of all Brutus stands to lose. Her loyalty stresses his fine spirit, which he is about to betray. Concentrating on Portia at this point rather than following Caesar shifts the action somewhat without lowering the tension. Suspense is maintained because Portia anxiously wants to know the same things the audience or reader wants to know.

Act III

21. **What is the purpose of the opening dialogue in Scene 1?**

These are not the long and measured speeches used throughout most of the play, but brief, disjointed questions and answers, jests, interruptions. Their staccato effect gives a sense of frenzied anticipation. The attempts to warn Caesar, the soothsayer's foreboding, the whispers of the conspirators prepare for the climactic moment of the killing.

22. **What is the final image of Caesar?**

Shakespeare draws an ironic and somewhat pathetic picture of the proud old man in his last moments. He orates at length about his own constancy, his refusal to change his mind (although he has just succumbed to the blandishments of Decius Brutus to attend the meeting). In the midst of a tribute to his own superiority, he is stricken down. The pathos is extended by the sense of betrayal: though Casca strikes the first blow, it is the treachery of his beloved friend Brutus which destroys him. His shocked "Et tu, Brute" ("You too, Brutus?") expresses his shattered trust in the once-honorable Brutus.

23. **How do the chief conspirators react to the deed?**

After the initial impact, both tend to undervalue the actual horror of destroying human life. Brutus, echoing Caesar's fatalism, disdains fear and insists on viewing the killing as a moral act. With their ritualistic blood-washing, they try to depict the death as a religious sacrifice to Roman freedom. (The blood-washing would have been performed on stage with some substitute for blood. The Elizabethans relished gore and violence, and Shakespeare would not have deleted these theatrics.) Cassius sees the death as the first step to new government; he predicts that history will remember them as patriots rather than killers.

24. **How do Cassius and Brutus approach Antony after the assassination?**

Cassius is pragmatic, intent on learning exactly where Antony stands, and whether his loyalties are transferable. He takes the initiative at once, asking a direct, businesslike question. His use of the word "prick'd" is an allusion to the knife-edge of Cassius' mind and foreshadows the scene in which the triumvirate "pricks" the names of their enemies for execution. The inference that Antony should be marked as an enemy is clear, but Brutus misses it completely.

When Antony asks that Brutus explain the killing, justify it, he appeals to Brutus' sense of reason. Brutus is putty in his hands. He seems anxious that Antony understand and assent in the murder. Perhaps he needs reassurance that his decision to kill Caesar was the right one; or perhaps he has so convinced himself that he is now sure of Antony's approval. Antony's show of measured grief — not too much, or the killers will think him intractable, not too little or they will find him unbelievable — completely take Brutus in.

25. **What is the significance of Brutus' decision to let Antony speak at the funeral?**

Again, Brutus is a poor judge of character. Just as Cassius had swayed him by guile, so Antony misleads him. Cassius is not deceived; he recognizes the ploy as a very dangerous one and argues that Antony should be denied the chance to speak. Yet Brutus has his way and seals the conspirator's doom. Giving Antony permission to speak is the turning point of the play. It shows Brutus' impractical idealism, his weakness in evaluating others, his incapacity to deal with guile. At this moment the conspirators have attained apparent success — Caesar is dead and his followers scattered — but Brutus makes the fatal decision which destroys his own cause.

26. **What portents appear in Antony's speech over Caesar's corpse?**

Speaking before the conspirators, he has carefully gauged the amount of grief he can show. Now, alone, before the crowd, he surrenders himself to the depth of his feeling. He vows revenge in bloody and passionate terms (an apocalyptic vision of the reign of terror later to descend on Rome); he denounces harmony, peace, all human feeling until vengeance can be exacted. The Elizabethan audience would have applauded this speech, rejecting regicide as a sacrilegious disruption of the chain of being. Antony's total control of himself is shown by quick return from emotional catharsis to pragmatic action. His message to Octavius is a complete turnabout from hot-blooded outcry to cold-blooded preparation.

27. Why does Brutus' speech fail?

Brutus believes he has justified his crime to Antony, and he uses the same argument in his speech to the populace. He claims justification for the killing in the name of patriotism and reason — "not that I lov'd Caesar less but that I lov'd Rome more." His speech is calm, balanced, and reasonable. His listeners accept it but are not swept away by it as they are by Antony's subsequent oration. Brutus asks the crowd to weigh his statements, to judge his reasons, but this requires thought and a grasp of the issues, much more difficult than a surrender to Antony's emotionalism. Brutus deals at the level of ideas and touches only their minds; Antony's dramatics capture their hearts.

28. What rhetorical device does Antony employ?

Until now Antony has been a lightweight. Caesar teased him about keeping late hours, Brutus saw him merely as an adjunct of the great Caesar, and he was generally regarded as a negligible playboy. Only Cassius recognized him as an antagonist. Apparently his bitterness and grief have transformed him, or at least hastened his development, into a strong-willed man, capable of deviousness and ruthless intellect. The speech is a virtuoso performance that utilizes Antony's superb grasp of crowd psychology. His masterful use of irony ensnares his listeners. They are forced to realize Antony means the opposite of what he says, and slowly they are overwhelmed by the thrust of his accusation.

He claims that he has not come to praise Caesar, but soon he is praising him vigorously for valor and virtue on behalf of Rome. He uses the word "honorable" so that the audience cannot escape the implication that the assassins are far from honorable indeed. He reminds his listeners that the conspirators have seized temporary control of Rome and that he speaks under their sufferance, knowing full well that such control denies the Roman ideals of justice and democracy. He says he must be careful not "to stir your hearts to mutiny and rage," although such stirring has already been done. Recognizing the unrest in the crowd, Antony makes a show of calming them, telling them that there is no reason to be aroused since they have not even heard about Caesar's will. After this bombshell, an element of curiosity and greed obsesses his audience. Antony neatly sidesteps their questions and heightens their excitement by showing Caesar's body, inciting not only their pity but their patriotism. Finally, knowing that their emotions are fully aroused, he proceeds to consolidate their feelings; he reveals that Caesar has left a legacy to all Rome. Antony is cynical enough to know that their emotionalism is not enough; they must be shown tangible proof of their best interest. The final incentive — monetary gain — commits them to an adherence to Caesar and a defiance of the conspirators.

29. **What is the purpose of Scene 4 between Cinna the Poet and the crowd?**

The actions of this crowd affirm the characterization of the masses in previous scenes. Casca has spoken contemptuously of the "tag-rag people"; Cassius has judged them so tractable that a well-regarded spokesman can fool them into overlooking a foul deed. Antony, at any rate, has found it easy enough to sway their emotions. Incensed, they attack the wrong man, exposing the chaotic disorder of Rome, the grim intentions of the populace, and the total failure of the conspirators. All this is in fulfillment of Antony's curse.

Act IV

30. **What new image of Antony emerges in Scene 1?**

Antony had grown during the funeral scene, assumed a new seriousness and strength. Now he gains another dimension. He is calculatingly cynical, ready to deprive the populace of the legacy which had so recently brought their allegiance. He is disloyal; he views Lepidus as unfit to be his partner, admitting he chose Lepidus only because he could use the man. Finally, all the emotion within him seems flown, used up in the storm of feeling caused by Caesar's death. He even consents to his nephew's execution. In his present obsession with power, such lack of feeling is necessary.

31. **How does the triumvirate compare to the conspirators?**

As rulers, they may be worse than the conspirators. They are ruthless, greedy, self-seeking, and power-hungry. Although Antony dominates the scene, Lepidus and Octavius agree with him on most matters of policy. However, they are the legitimate successors to Caesar. Even as bloody avengers, they have a legal right to rule that the assassins can never claim.

32. **What does the quarrel between Cassius and Brutus reveal?**

Act IV must allow no drop in tension between the high point in Act III and the final resolution in Act V. Thus the horror of the reign of terror in Rome, as shown in the preceding scene and discussed by the conspirators in Scene 2, adds to the tension. The conspirators' quarrel not only maintains emotion at a high pitch, but shows the disintegration of the conspiracy.

It also reinforces the qualities of Brutus and Cassius which have been established in earlier acts. Cassius has strength and drive but is flawed by a basic pettiness. He would stoop to accepting bribes in the midst of their campaign. Brutus, on the other hand, is flawed by an impracticality in dealing with reality. For surely, at such a crucial moment, there is a more diplomatic way to negotiate the details of fund raising. Although Brutus is clearly right to object to corruption, he has chosen the wrong moment and the wrong manner. One need only remember the cool restraint of the triumvirate to gauge with accuracy the ultimate victors.

33. **What effect is gained by the revelation of Portia's death?**

The news of Portia's death, and its gruesome manner, creates sympathy for Brutus. Even Cassius forgets the bitterness of their quarrel and a rapport is reestablished. Now it seems that Brutus has reached his nadir in contrast to his former state. He was an honored citizen with a noble wife, a long tradition of family prestige, and the high regard of his country; now he has sunk to the status of hunted outlaw.

34. **What lingering effects does the quarrel have?**

Brutus realizes that Cassius is flawed, and that he himself has been misled in accepting the leadership of such a man. The hollowness of their "mission" is now clear to him. Are such petty, bickering plotters as they more fit to rule Rome than Caesar? For the first time he learns to assess character correctly and wonders whether he and Cassius were mistaken in trying to replace Caesar. He no longer believes in the ultimate justice of their cause. A final aftermath of the quarrel is that Cassius seals the reconciliation by allowing Brutus to plan the battle strategy. High price, indeed, for the "prestige" he has bought with Brutus.

35. **What is the purpose of the appearance of the ghost?**

First, such a spectre was a crowd-pleaser in Shakespeare's day; the audience believed in ghosts and omens, and a phantom was a desirable theatrical convention. Secondly, it is vital that the link between cause and effect be established, that Caesar's murder — for which Brutus is about to die — be remembered. When the ghost introduces himself as "thy evil spirit, Brutus," it is to remind Brutus that the evil in his own nature caused his present plight. In the interim since Caesar's death, the opposing sides both seem unfit to rule, so it is important that the moral issue underlying the political be restated. Finally, the ghost's threat to reappear at Philippi increases the anticipatory tension and points to a final dramatic solution.

Act V

36. **How does Antony appear in Scene 1?**

He is a man in complete control of the situation. Confident that his spies have informed him accurately, he is pleased to see his enemy's tactics playing into his hands. Again the cool confidence of the triumvirate seems to show the victor.

37. **What is the importance of the characterization of Octavius?**

Although the drama would be complete of itself, the audience is aware of the historical facts behind it. And those facts show Octavius as the final victor, defeating Antony and installing himself as first in a dynasty of imperial Caesars. So, even though his part in this drama is brief, Octavius attracts attention. Though his lines are few, they are all the more weighted.

He has made a rather unsavory beginning in Act IV, Scene 1, where he proposes the execution of Lepidus' brother. Although Antony makes a similar ruthless impression, the audience has seen him weep over Caesar's body and curse the murderers. Thus Antony's ruthlessness seems somehow justified, while Octavius has shown no "sympathetic" side to balance his coldness. In the present scene his characterization continues along the same lines; even in the face of their approaching victory, he cannot resist the chance to say "I told you so" to Antony. Then a final spat over battle strategy ends with Octavius' ominous comment, "I do not cross you; but I will do so." That Octavius gives the play's final speech is another allusion to Octavius' ultimate victory.

38. **What is the purpose of the parley between the two sides?**

It seems to serve little strategic purpose except to give them a chance to exchange insults, flaunt their bravery, and whet their appetites for war. After they retire to their side, Cassius and Brutus cheer each other on, or try to. Cassius poignantly reveals that it is his birthday, implying his knowledge that it will also be his death day. Try as they will to encourage one another, each has had omens of defeat and is resigned to the outcome.

39. **How does Cassius die?**

Believing the battle lost and his friend Titinius taken, he asks his slave to kill him. As Brutus is to do shortly after, he devotes his last words to Julius Caesar, so that the circle of action-reaction is closed. His soldiers then return to tell him, ironically, that all is lost, the battle still in doubt; but his own assumption of defeat has quickened his doom. The last appraisal of Cassius is softened by the tears of Brutus. He knows Cassius is a flawed but still beloved friend, recalls his strengths and virtues. The spirit of Julius Caesar is now avenged.

40. **What final evaluation is given of Brutus?**

Again he is shown as pragmatically inept; he had selected the disastrous battle site, and now he gives the signal at the wrong time, ensuring confusion and defeat. His old nobility is reaffirmed, however, in the refusal of his friends to kill him, and he marvels at their loyalty. Finally, choosing death rather than dishonor, he runs upon a sword. When his body is found by the opposing leaders, the final appraisal is a mellowed one. Both Antony and Octavius eulogize him heartily, commend his motives in the assassination, and promise him honorable rites. Antony restores him to his respected stature and he dies "the noblest Roman of them all."

The Play's the Thing: Discussion Questions

Motivation:

1. **What is Brutus' original image of his own morality?**

Brutus is somewhat self-deceived. His is a nobility which apparently has not been sufficiently tested by challenge. To himself, as well as to the Roman people at large, he seems a highly moral man. He has attained this stature through generations of public-spirited ancestors and through his own behavior. Although reluctant to resort to assassination, he has enough confidence in his own view of what is good for the state to make the crucial decision. In doing so he places his morality above the universal code of good and evil.

2. **How does his self-image change?**

Brutus comes to a rude awakening when the act of assassination results not only in condemnation and chastisement (they are forced to flee Rome and fight for their lives) but in a realization that the "cause" was not a true one. He finds his cohorts unworthy, and their actions in the name of Roman justice have resulted in an oppressive tyranny for his beloved homeland. Brutus has misjudged not only the nature of his acts but the outcome of his deeds.

3. How does Brutus' attitude toward Cassius change?

Brutus' inability to evaluate Cassius accurately is a symptom of his general incapacity to judge human nature, a foreshadowing of his blunder in permitting Antony to speak at Caesar's funeral. Brutus views Cassius as a fine man with honest reasons for desiring Caesar's death, and allows himself to be convinced by the other's specious arguments. Later, disillusioned by the failure of the conspirators to hold power in Rome, he is aghast to learn of Cassius' taking bribes. While some might consider this a small offense, it proves the man's corruption and offends Brutus to the core. Their argument is smoothed over, however, and they go into battle reconciled. At his death Brutus can mourn for him, willing to accept the man flawed as he is. Just as Brutus now regrets his own godlike judgment that Caesar should die, he no longer insists on godlike virtue in others. He sees Cassius as a human being not perfect, yet with some virtues to appreciate.

4. How does Brutus underestimate Antony?

From the beginning Brutus tends to discount Antony. He knows him as "quick" but underrates his loyalty and ability. His decisions to allow Antony to live and to speak at the funeral are based on this insulting appraisal. He believes Antony powerless without Caesar's guidance, and he feels that he himself will have greater public influence than Antony. He soon sees how wrong his judgment is. After Antony erupts at the funeral, shows his true loyalty, and exerts his full powers, Brutus realizes too late the strength of his adversary.

5. **How does Brutus change his opinion about the need for Caesar's death?**

At the beginning he bases his opinion about the danger in Caesar's ambition upon unfounded, conditional reasoning. His decision is not based upon facts but upon possibilities. Seeing the ascension of a triumvirate more ruthless and tyrannical than Caesar ever was, he realizes the error of his thinking. Also, the revelation of the true character of the conspirators and their motives disillusions him. By the end of the drama he regrets his part in Caesar's murder, realizing that no moral end can ever result from an immoral act.

Philosophy:

1. **What is Shakespeare's view of the relationship between man and society?**

Man and society were related as part of the "great chain of being." Individual man had to function properly *within his own sphere* as part of universal order. It was just as important for a cobbler to do his best and maintain his station in life as it was for a king. Man owes obedience to the best within himself and can achieve it by being faithful to his place in society. To Shakespeare and his contemporaries, citizens of a country that had been torn by a series of bloody civil wars, nothing was more abhorrent than the attempt to take by force a station higher than one's rightful place. The sin of *hubris* — overwe'ening pride manifested in ambition that knows no bounds — is anathema to social order, and this sin will be punished. Brutus, apparently obeying the dictates of conscience, is actually no better than Cassius, who operates out of envious spite. They both join in the unlawful disposition of a ruler and an attempt to take his place. In Tudor England disruption of the status quo was a heinous crime.

2. **What is Shakespeare's view of the relationship between man and nature?**

Just as man was part of society, so was human society interconnected with nature in the great chain of being. Harmony in the universe was based on the interdependence of all its phases. A break in the chain at any level caused reverberations throughout. Thus when the conspirators plan the regicide, all nature protests. Frightening storms occur, oceans swell up, and night birds shriek at midday; unnatural apparitions abound — lions walking Rome's streets, dead men risen, and other horrifying manifestations. For every human act is of far-reaching consequence and involves not only man's individual conscience but his society and the world of nature at large.

3. **Does Shakespeare believe that man is punished for the evil he does, rewarded for the good?**

This question of punishment and reward is at the core of all religions and philosophies and seems ultimately unanswerable. Like that of any thinking man at pains to make philosophy consistent with human experience, Shakespeare's answer must be somewhat ambiguous. While there is no clear-cut system of reward and punishment, man's actions are taken into account in the end. Evil is usually punished, and though a good man may suffer, virtue is usually considered a blessing in itself. Brutus commits an immoral act and is punished for it by losing everything he values — his beloved wife, his homeland, his stature as an honorable citizen, his own self-image as a man of integrity, and finally his very life. But in suffering he gains new understanding of himself and his acts. Thus suffering becomes a catalyst for development and growth and he dies a better man for it.

4. **If there is no clear-cut relationship between morality and reward, sin and punishment, what forces do determine man's fate?**

Shakespeare had a strong belief in Fortune, a power that interfered with and in many cases greatly affected human activities. His plays are full of coincidences, mishaps, and misunderstandings, like the accident of Cassius' failure to understand Brutus' change of battle tactics at Philippi. In the main, life is a mystery to man, who is often affected by indescribable forces against which he is powerless. However, a belief in fate does not deprive man of his will. Man has the will to act, to take a moral stand (as Brutus does, even if mistakenly), and even in suffering to become a finer person through self-knowledge.

Politics in Action:

1. **What three types of revolutionary leaders do Brutus, Antony, and Cassius exemplify?**

Brutus is honorable and unrealistic, the man who activates forces he cannot control. He is an idealist who fails to understand the true nature of political action, more at home with grandiose ideas than with real situations. He is a decent man, the type whose philosophy often engenders revolutionary action, but who becomes a figurehead when the cause develops and gains momentum through the actions of others.

Cassius is the hard-boiled pragmatist, motivated by personal ambition or envy rather than by idealism. He is a shrewd appraiser of others and knows how to employ their weaknesses as well as strengths. Motivated by less than noble ends, he is at least capable of dealing with reality.

Antony is the classic rabble-rouser. Although his original motives may have been pure, once he has gained power he is less like Brutus, more like Cassius. He uses a variety of demagogic tricks to whip the crowd into a frenzy and possesses a masterful grasp of mob psychology. While Brutus misunderstands reality and Cassius seeks to falsify reality, Antony utilizes reality to gain his own ends. He is capable of weeping over Caesar's death in all sincerity and then, with equal sincerity, planning his own nephew's death and urging the elimination of Lepidus. To him the main issue is all that matters. Once Caesar is dead, destroying the conspirators and seizing power for himself comprise the main issue.

2. **What evaluation of "the mob" emerges from the play?**

From the first, the crowd is viewed an as animal which can be coerced, hoodwinked, or manipulated. The mob is fickle, easily swayed by oratory, highly emotional, and greedy. They have power, brute power, but no real rights. Rome is less a democracy than an oligarchy; the conspirators do not fear that the common citizens may lose their liberties under Caesar, but that they themselves, Rome's aristocrats, will lose influence. The conspirators view the populace as "the common herd," a group who will accept murder if smoothed over by a cover-up. The estimate by the opposing triumvirate is not much better. Octavius and Antony, who have come to power by manipulating popular emotion, are unconcerned with popular rights and immediately seek to deprive the people of Caesar's legacy, so prominent in their accession to power.

3. **If Brutus and Cassius are the villains of the drama, by virtue of the fact that they commit a deed obviously considered immoral by Shakespeare, does this mean that their rivals — the triumvirate — thus become the heroes of the play?**

The moral calibre of Antony and Octavius is revealed as about the same as Cassius' and greatly inferior to Brutus'. This is one of the ironic points which Shakespeare emphasizes: the killing of Caesar is not only sinful but futile, since a more totalitarian government emerges than the one they feared. However, right is on the side of the triumvirate, since they represent the triumph of order. They act as heirs to Caesar, and possess the virtue of legitimacy, power passed down the channels of legality. There is no clear-cut hero in this play; the finer nature of Brutus is the "hero" and the drama's tragedy is that he allows the baser nature of himself and others to overcome his finer side. The final words of Antony praising the dead Brutus show that he is the potential, if not actual, hero.

4. **While preparing for a battle which may be decisive to their cause, Brutus charges Cassius with accepting bribes. Is his insistence on dealing with the matter at this time evidence of Brutus' morality or of his ineptness?**

Responses here may vary. Students should be encouraged to consider the ramifications of their answers. What use are the traits of "good leadership" if a man lacks power? Is Cassius not then justified in doing everything he can to assume power? What good is Brutus' nobility if arguing over petty matters prevents him from winning power? Is immorality ever "petty"? Discuss real-life examples of corruption in government, whether on the municipal, state, or national level, and determine their effect on the good of the state, as well as on the persons involved.

Encore: Vocabulary Words

The main words in the groups below are taken from *Julius Caesar*. Mark the letter of the word that comes closest in meaning to each main word.

Act I

1. tributaries
   a. habits
   b. subordinates
   c. tricks

2. servile
   a. subservient
   b. wise
   c. cruel

3. construe
   a. scatter
   b. build
   c. interpret

4. cogitations
   a. movements
   b. thoughts
   c. places

5. accoutred
   a. equipped
   b. constructed
   c. painted

6. encompass
   a. direct
   b. support
   c. surround

7. loath
   a. hate
   b. reluctant
   c. small

8. prodigious
   a. childlike
   b. changing
   c. extraordinary

9. redress
   a. make amends for
   b. problem
   c. wardrobe

10. infirmity
    a. envy
    b. weakness
    c. accident

Act II

11. augment
    a. charm
    b. starve
    c. increase

12. insurrection
    a. rudeness
    b. rebellion
    c. indefinite

13. affability
    a. carelessness
    b. capacity
    c. amiability

14. visage
    a. thrift
    b. vision
    c. face

15. augurer
    a. one who predicts
    b. one who serves
    c. one who betrays

16. fray
    a. jealousy
    b. repair
    c. brawl

17. dank
    a. bowl
    b. disagreeably moist
    c. mirage

18. vile
    a. evil
    b. bottle
    c. pair

19. constancy
    a. yearning
    b. faithfulness
    c. remedy

20. chide
    a. scold
    b. youngster
    c. burn

Act III

21. puissant
    a. possible
    b. mighty
    c. careless

22. firmament
    a. ground
    b. strength
    c. heavens

23. abridged
    a. shortened
    b. accepted
    c. refused

24. grievous
    a. superstitious
    b. dead
    c. severe

25. arbor
    a. dark
    b. retain
    c. garden

26. extenuated
    a. diminished
    b. forgiven
    c. flattered

27. bondman
    a. warrant
    b. slave
    c. superior

28. prostrate
   a. lying face down
   b. suffering
   c. vow

29. enfranchise
   a. deny
   b. trust
   c. liberate

30. unassailable
   a. correct
   b. invincible
   c. insignificant

Act IV

31. provender
   a. provider
   b. seller
   c. animal food

32. covert
   a. hidden
   b. ditch
   c. maneuver

33. choleric
   a. hot-tempered
   b. overweight
   c. priest

34. waspish
   a. tiny
   b. disagreeable
   c. intense

35. apparition
   a. phantom
   b. evidence
   c. warning

36. testy
   a. cursed
   b. repaired
   c. irritable

37. taper
   a. pressure
   b. candle
   c. resist

38. vexed
   a. angered
   b. questioned
   c. courteous

39. insupportable
   a. unique
   b. unbearable
   c. casual

40. chastisement
   a. punishment
   b. probability
   c. discovery

Act V

41. cur
   a. abrupt
   b. mongrel
   c. groom

42. demeanour
   a. unpleasant
   b. lesser
   c. bearing or behavior

43. perceive
   a. understand
   b. accept
   c. labor

44. tarry
   a. marvel
   b. wait
   c. misunderstanding

45. suffice
   a. entertain
   b. material
   c. satisfy

46. presage
   a. foreshadow
   b. gift
   c. grudge

47. peevish
   a. unclean
   b. fretful
   c. brief

48. apt
   a. suitable
   b. industrious
   c. sincere

49. engendered
   a. wise
   b. produced
   c. dreaded

50. garland
   a. wreath
   b. loud
   c. orchard

Improvisation: Student Enrichment

Research:

1. Shakespeare based *Julius Caesar* on the account in Plutarch's *Lives*. Check this book and note the ways in which Shakespeare has expanded and enlivened the characters without altering the essential facts.

2. Organize a debate on this question. Resolved: that Cassius, with his petty motivation but superior efficiency, would have made a better ruler than Brutus, whose ideals were high but who was ineffectual in dealing with reality.

3. Using the reference section of your library, write an account of one of the following political leaders assassinated by those who disagreed with their ideology: Trujillo, of the Dominican Republic;

Masaryk, of Czechoslovakia; Lincoln, of the United States; Allende, of Chile; and Ferdinand, of Austria.

Reaction:

1. The conspirator Brutus believed that the immoral act of murder would in this case benefit all Romans. Do you agree that a noble end sometimes justifies less than noble means?

2. Shakespeare uses great insight to show the contrast between how a character sees himself and how he really is. Do you notice a similar contrast in people you know?

3. The qualities of leadership are discussed from various angles throughout the play. Write a brief essay about the qualities you feel are necessary for leadership. Are they the same qualities which ensure the assumption of power?

4. Suppose that the assassination plot had been discovered and Caesar had lived. Would he have changed Rome as Brutus feared? Would Brutus have been punished for his part in the plot?

Imagination:

1. Write a short synopsis of the ending of the play had Mark Antony not spoken at the funeral. Would the Romans have accepted the justification for the assassination? Could the conspirators have built a workable government? Would it have been less tyrannical than the one formed by the triumvirate?

2. Write a newspaper account of the events that occurred at Caesar's funeral, an account to be published that day in Rome.

3. Draw up a series of posters for a mock Roman election.

What qualities would you ascribe to each of the following — Mark Antony, Julius Caesar, Brutus, and Cassius?

4. Script-write or role-play a conversation between Antony and a friend in which Antony explains his strategy in meeting the conspirators and convincing them to permit him to speak at Caesar's funeral.

Between the Lines: Essay Test

Literal Level

1. What is the turning point of the play?

2. Why is Brutus necessary to the conspiracy?

3. Name three qualities of Antony and give examples of them in his words or deeds.

Interpretive Level

1. Name three qualities of "the mob" and show how Antony works with each quality in his funeral oration.

2. Contrast Cassius and Brutus.

3. Who is the protagonist in the play? Explain why.

4. What is the turning point in the play?

Final Curtain: Objective Test

I. True—False

Mark each statement T for True or F for False.

_____ 1. Brutus admits he lacks Antony's "quick spirit."

_____ 2. Brutus' main motive in killing Caesar is spite for an old injury Caesar had done him.

_____ 3. Brutus is better at dealing with vague ideas than with real people and situations.

_____ 4. Alchemy means the process of shaping gold into beautiful objects.

_____ 5. Brutus contends that Caesar's death is necessary to stop his ambition.

_____ 6. Cassius mostly opposes Caesar on political principles.

_____ 7. The "bathing-in-blood" scene was realistically performed on the Elizabethan stage because the audience loved gore and violence.

_____ 8. Antony's grief for Caesar is sincere since he speaks of it in a soliloquy by Caesar's body.

_____ 9. Caesar's cry "Et tu, Brute" means "Help me, Brutus!"

_____10. Brutus convinces Cassius that Antony should be allowed to live.

_____11. The anonymous letters that Brutus receives are not genuine.

_____12. Brutus never regrets the killing of Caesar.

_____13. Mark Antony shows hypocrisy when he tries to deprive the Roman public of their legacy.

_____14. The storms before Caesar's death are omens of an unnatural act to come.

_____15. Caesar's ghost appears to both Brutus and Cassius.

II. Multiple Choice

Choose the best answer to complete each statement.

16. Brutus views the assassination as a sacrifice to
    a. his own ambition.
    b. the liberty of Rome.
    c. his friendship with Cassius.

17. Brutus says the plotters need no oath because
    a. it is too late.
    b. they are bound by a cause, not empty words.
    c. they have already sworn one.

18. The quarrel between Brutus and Cassius at camp near Sardis shows
    a. how the conspiracy is disintegrating.
    b. Brutus' growing ability to deal with practical problems.
    c. Cassius' ability to manipulate Brutus.

19. Octavius and Antony form a triumvirate with
    a. Lepidus.
    b. Flavius.
    c. Ligarius.

20. Brutus' wife
    a. joins him at the end of the play.
    b. betrays him to Antony.
    c. is Cato's daughter.

21. Caesar does not fear death because
    a. he thinks himself immortal.
    b. it must come to all men.
    c. the soothsayer tells him all is well.

22. The drama's turning point is
    a. Brutus' decision to join the conspiracy.
    b. the killing of Caesar.
    c. Brutus' decision to let Antony speak at the funeral.

23. The triumvirate seems
    a. cold and ruthless.
    b. anxious to preserve Roman justice.
    c. a close-knit alliance.

24. The Roman mob reacts to Antony's sarcastic use of the word
    a. "Roman."
    b. "honorable."
    c. "friendship."

25. The play opens at a
    a. public holiday.
    b. private religious service.
    c. funeral.

26. Cassius compares Brutus to "metal" because
    a. he is wealthy.
    b. he is a famous soldier.
    c. his honor seems stiff but can be molded.

27. Caesar says he does not trust
    a. Brutus.
    b. Antony.
    c. Cassius.

28. In their last talk Brutus convinces Cassius
    a. to move to Philippi.
    b. to fight at Sardis.
    c. to call a truce.

29. The day of the final battle is
    a. the Ides of March.
    b. Brutus' birthday.
    c. Cassius' birthday.

30. Brutus dies
    a. at the hands of Antony.
    b. on his own sword.
    c. in a quarrel with Cassius.

31. Caesar's wife warns him
    a. of her ominous dreams.
    b. to beware of Cassius.
    c. to be careful of Antony.

32. The scene between Cinna the Poet and the mob shows
    a. how Cinna uses his brains to save his life.
    b. the senseless anger of the mob at the conspirators.
    c. how Brutus saves a friend.

33. Brutus is disturbed when the conspirators
    a. arrive under cover of darkness.
    b. join with Antony.
    c. involve his wife in the conspiracy.

34. Caesar never displays
    a. arrogance.
    b. physical infirmity.
    c. greed.

35. Cassius needs Brutus in the plot because of
    a. his fine reputation.
    b. his fine swordsmanship.
    c. his financial backing.

III. Matching

Match the characters with proper descriptions.

_____36. Brutus
_____37. Caesar
_____38. Portia
_____39. Cassius
_____40. Calpurnia

    a. Brutus' wife
    b. Caesar's wife
    c. Suffers from "falling sickness"
    d. Convinces Brutus to join plot
    e. Called "the noblest Roman"

_____41. Antony
_____42. Artemidorus
_____43. Marullus
_____44. Octavius
_____45. Pompey

    a. Caesar's nephew
    b. Roman leader before Caesar
    c. Tries to warn Caesar
    d. Agrees to own nephew's death
    e. Roman tribune

    a.   Joins plot because of Brutus

    b.   First to stab Caesar

    c.   Convinces Caesar to attend Senate

    d.   Brutus' servant

    e.   Wrote history of Julius Caesar

A Small Account
of the Grandeur that was Rome

Thousands of words have been written about Rome.
These words have been presented as massive tomes such
as *The Decline and Fall of the Roman Empire*. There
have been novels and drama. And song and poetry.

The following simplified micro-course is provided as an
easy-to-read capsule of that fascinating era in the history
of the world. The hope would be that, after this simple
introduction, the reader will be encouraged to approach
the Pierian spring and drink more deeply.

EARLY ROME

The city of Rome is in a part of the continent of Europe
called Italy. Italy is a long peninsula which looks like a
boot. Rome is in the middle of Italy on the west side.
Like most old cities, Rome is on a river. Rome's river is
the Tiber.

The people who lived in and around the city of Rome
about 27 B.C. were called Latins. The Latins soon came

to be dominated by the Etruscans. The Etruscans ruled the Latins and the city of Rome for almost 200 years. The Latins came to resent the Etruscans, and finally drove them out. The Latins were now free to rule themselves.

The people of Rome began to invade neighboring countries and take over their lands. As Rome usurped more land, the city of Rome also made enemies. One of these enemies was the city of Carthage.

Rome fought three wars with Carthage. These wars were called the Punic Wars. The Punic Wars lasted for many years. Finally, Rome defeated Carthage and the people of Carthage were taken as slaves. Rome also took all the land of Carthage.

LIFE INSIDE ROME

In the city of Rome there were two classes of people. There were the very rich and the very poor. The rich people were called Patricians. The poor people were called Plebians.

The Patricians were powerful and controlled the government. The Plebians had very little power. They were relegated to serving in the Roman armies without pay. The Patricians ultimately acquired all the land that Rome took in the past from Carthage.

After the Punic Wars, three men ruled the Roman Empire. Rule by three men is called a "triumvirate." The First Triumvirate was made up of Pompey, Julius Caesar, and a third man, Marcus Crassus. Each man ruled a part of the Roman Empire. Soon, Pompey and Julius Caesar started to quarrel. Pompey was killed. Ultimately, Julius Caesar ruled Rome alone. But Julius Caesar was not well liked. As a result, he was assassinated in a plot filled with intrigue.

After Julius Caesar was killed, Rome was ruled by the Second Triumvirate. The Second Triumvirate was made up of Marc Antony, Octavian (the nephew of Julius Caesar), and Lepidus. Marc Antony set out on an expedition to Egypt. There he fell in love with Cleopatra, the Queen of Egypt.

Marc Antony and Cleopatra wanted to rule all of

Rome, so their armies attacked Octavian. Marc Antony was defeated, leaving Octavian to rule Rome and all its lands. Marc Antony and Cleopatra took their own lives.

IMPERIAL ROME

Now that Octavian ruled all of Rome and its lands, there was a long peace. The peace lasted for more than 200 years. This period was called Pax Romana. Pax Romana means "Roman Peace." The citizens were happy because it was the end of civil wars. People bestowed on Octavian the title of Augustus Caesar. The word "Augustus" indicated a person with much power.

After Augustus died, his adopted son became ruler of Rome. The son's name was Tiberius. Tiberius was not a popular ruler. He lived away from Rome on the island of Capri off the coast of what is now Italy. The Roman people were unhappy because they expected the emperor to live in Rome.

After the mysterious death of Tiberius, Caligula ruled Rome. Caligula was the great-nephew of Tiberius. Caligula was not a good ruler, either, and was regarded as eccentric. He was finally killed by his own soldiers. The soldiers made Claudius the next ruler of Rome. Claudius was Caligula's uncle.

Claudius was a good ruler. He made Britain part of the Roman Empire. Nevertheless, there were many attempts on his life. Claudius was finally poisoned, and Nero became ruler of Rome. Nero was Claudius' son. Some Romans believed that Nero's mother poisoned Claudius so her son could become emperor.

Nero was another failure as a ruler. He was also an eccentric. On occasion, he would dress up in lion skins and scare children. Nero even killed his own mother because he disliked her so much.

Nero disliked Christians, too. For amusement, he put them in the Colosseum to battle lions. The Colosseum was a big arena, much like a football stadium. The Romans had contests and races there. Some historians believe Nero set fire to Rome. Finally, the people tried to kill Nero, but he killed himself first. Nero was the last person from the Caesar family to rule Rome.

After the Caesar family, there were many other rulers of Rome. Some of the important rulers:

★ **Hadrian** was a first-rate ruler. He built a famous wall in Britain to defend against invaders from the North.

★ **Marcus Aurelius** ruled Rome for over nineteen years. He was also a writer. He wrote a book called *The Meditations.*

★ **Diocletian** was a strong ruler. He divided the Roman Empire into two parts—the Western Roman Empire and the Eastern Roman Empire. He expected people to consider him a god.

★ **Constantine** started a new city. It was called Constantinople after Constantine. It was almost as important as Rome.

THE FALL OF ROME

The Roman Empire was beset with problems. The problems sparked the end of the Roman Empire. Problems were both internal and external.

The problems inside the empire were between the rich and the poor. The poor faced unemployment because the rich owned slaves. The slaves did all the work. As a result, the poor people were given bread so they would not starve and circuses so they would not get bored. But even these diversions did not keep the poor from becoming restless.

The problems outside of the empire were caused by the Huns from the north. One group of Huns was called the Visigoths. The Romans let the Huns live in the Roman Empire. But soon the Visigoths fought the Romans because they had been mistreated by the Romans. The Visigoths defeated the Romans.

Then other Huns, such as the Vandals and the Lombards, started to invade the Roman Empire. After 476, the Roman Empire no longer existed.

ROME'S ACCOMPLISHMENTS

Rome did many fine things for the world. Here are some of the things Rome did:

★ Rome gave us Christianity. Christ was born into the Roman Empire. At first, the Romans persecuted the Christians. But later, the Emperor Constantine became a Christian, and Tiberius made Christianity the only religion of the Roman Empire.

★ Rome built many fine things. Some of them, like the Colosseum, still stand today.

★ The Romans left the world their language. The Romans spoke Latin. Many of our languages come from Latin. English uses many words which were once Latin. French, Spanish, Italian, and Portuguese are languages that come from Latin. They are called Romance Languages from the word "Rome."